T0129296

ESCAPE
TO
NOWHERE

ESCAPE
TO
NOWHERE

Ron Reynolds...The Only Yank to Escape
from the French Foreign Legion

As told to
FRAN LUCCA

ESCAPE TO NOWHERE
RON REYNOLDS...THE ONLY YANK TO ESCAPE FROM THE FRENCH FOREIGN LEGION

iUniverse books may be ordered through booksellers or by contacting:

iUniverse
1663 Liberty Drive
Bloomington, IN 47403
www.iuniverse.com
1-800-Authors (1-800-288-4677)

ISBN: 978-1-5320-7772-2 (sc)
ISBN: 978-1-5320-7773-9 (e)

Print information available on the last page.

iUniverse rev. date: 08/05/2019

DEDICATION

This book is dedicated to the late Kenmore East High School history teacher Robert Reppenhagen, whose intense research into the French Foreign Legion made this all possible.

CHAPTER 1

The American jazz music played by the German combo didn't help lift my spirits. After more than a year of wandering throughout the States, and then Europe, I still hadn't shaken that insatiable impulse from my system. I guess it was there, in West Berlin's *"Die Badewanne"* nightclub on a September evening in 1956, sitting with Kurt and the two girls, that I finally made up my mind to join the French Foreign Legion.

Kurt tried hard to lift me out of the dumps.

"Ronnie, my comrade, why are you so sad?"

"Sorry Kurt, maybe I'm homesick. After all it's been several months since I was back home."

"Well, tonight we drink and make merry."

"Yeah, sure"

"No, no Ronnie, you are too much the fatalist. Why do you not dance with Lisa?"

Lisa was a gorgeous brunette, about 18, and with the vital statistics of a Miss Universe. I couldn't speak German, and she couldn't speak English, but I don't think we would have had a difficult time communicating.

"Kurt, tell Lisa that I'm not up to dancing."

Lisa got the message and pouted. Then she whispered something to Olga, a blonde chunky girl. Both of them giggled and got up to dance together.

Kurt ordered another pitcher of beer. "What are you going to do now, Ronnie, go back to the boats?"

"No, I had enough of swab jockey life on the Norwegian ship."

"Well, then, why not stay here in Berlin with me, and I can get you a job at my newspaper?"

"Thanks Kurt, but I think I'll take in Paris next."

The combo tore into a Dixieland number, and the tempo reached a fever pitch. Looking around the night spot, I recognized the pictures of more than a dozen American jazz greats: Satchmo, Goodman, Ellington, etc. The club got its name *"Badewanne,"* which means bathtub, from the sunken dance floor.

Two men joined our table and Lisa and Olga returned to join in the festive singing. I went through the motions, but my heart wasn't in it. The happier everyone got, the sadder I became. Somehow I couldn't go along with all the gaiety. Maybe it was because I couldn't spend any money and was dressed for traveling, not dancing.

The two men finally grabbed our dates and swept them out onto the dance floor. We didn't see any of them again.

"Sorry I'm such a wet blanket Kurt, but I guess I've got other things in mind."

"Don't apologize my friend. It was good of you to stop by and see me on your way to France."

As the German beer seeped alcohol into my bloodstream, my thinking became mellow and nostalgic. I thought I was seeing things more clearly, although actually my mental vision was mildly blurred by the drinks. I began to think fate had caused me to be a man without roots, not at home in America, and only an onlooker in Berlin.

It had always been my weakness and conceit to feel a bit apart in a group, especially after a couple of drinks. Philosophical ideas chased around in my mind, and again I had the familiar thought that if I could catch and pin down one of these vagaries, I would have the answer to many riddles of my relationship with the rest of the world.

What was I doing so far from home, I asked myself. I had come to Berlin to visit a friend, but I was really searching for some meaning to my life. Pushed to the back of my mind was a quixotic desire to join the French Foreign Legion. On the one hand, the idea was frightening, but on the other it had a morbid fascination, a mystical belief that it would provide me with the ultimate reality.

"A *pfennig* for your thoughts," Kurt cut into my daydreaming.

I smiled. "Why is it that everyone else seems to be have a good time while I sit on the side lines?"

"Don't get so serious," Kurt rejoined. "I had enough realities in the war and now I just accept things."

Kurt had served under Rommel in Africa and had been captured in Italy. He carried with him a crippled arm as his souvenir of Hitler's Reich.

I had met Kurt for the first time in Stockholm. We were both tourists and I think Kurt took to me because I obviously was traveling on a shoestring. I toured European style to get more mileage for my money and met Kurt on a boat, which was the youth hostel in Stockholm. This ship was anchored in the harbor for sleeping, and not traveling.

At the time I didn't expect to ever see Kurt again. We had been introduced and a group of us had walked through the city doing some sightseeing. Kurt seemed to get a kick out of my comments, which reflected a disillusioned, meager youth.

Later, sometime after I left Stockholm, Kurt had written to my home in the U.S. and obtained my address in the Norwegian Merchant Marine. We corresponded and eventually I decided to accept Kurt's invitation to visit him in his home city. I had hesitated partly because of the difficulty of getting to Berlin. Some travelers had told me that it was very difficult to obtain a permit to cross East German territory and so most people flew in. Airplanes were not in my budget.

I started on the trip, seeing it as something of a challenge. I hitchhiked to the border of East Germany and managed to obtain a special Russian visa. My luck continued when I got a free ride on a bus to Berlin. This vehicle was deadheading back to Berlin after carrying Volkswagen drivers from the old capital to the factory in West Berlin.

Kurt was an efficient German who arranged all of my housekeeping details. This morning he had shown me through the newspaper office where he worked at laying out ads. Work was put aside while my German friend introduced me to the office girls, and then found me a bed in a youth hostel. Kurt seemed to be shaping up as a real friend.

After getting set in the hostel, I wandered about the Western area while Kurt returned to his work. In the early evening we had dinner across from the zoo at the Zoo Train Station, a low cost restaurant where you can eat all you want for a couple of marks, or about a half-dollar. It bothered me somewhat to have someone else pay the bill, but I had come this far on a strict budget which called for about twenty-five cents a meal.

All of this ran through my mind as I sat in the nightclub. My original plan was to stay in Berlin a month or two and then head for Southern Europe for the winter, continuing my travels on a tight pocket book. Gradually though, this Legion notion was popping up in the back of my mind.

All of these people having a good time struck me as victims of an illusion, of foolish and futile activity. Perhaps they might be adjusted, but I wasn't. A normal life of work and family was fine, but not for me, not yet. My thoughts went back to all my wanderings and experiences, and still it seemed something had been eluding me. I was nineteen years old and wanted to get this restlessness out of me before settling down.

Back in Buffalo, my normal middle-class family was wondering how they had produced such a maverick. I felt I had to push this thing through to some kind of conclusion before I went back to suburbia.

My thoughts drifted back to my first touch of wanderlust, just over four years ago. I had gone by bicycle from Buffalo to Washington, D.C. I recalled wryly that at first I was homesick and ready to abandon traveling for good.

Now travel itself was too routine. I craved adventure that the average individual had not tasted. Often I had dreamed of the fabulous French Foreign Legion, but now it was time to act. I swore to myself that tomorrow morning I was going to begin putting this dream into reality. I knew things appeared bleaker on the morning after, but I resolved to force myself to go on.

I patted my crotch, because there was my treasure- all my cash that I had saved up that summer working in the Norwegian Merchant Marine. This seemed a safe place. I had made my own money belt from an old jock strap and a couple of old pants pockets. I called it my grouch bag. I was banking on this money to carry me through six months of winter in Southern Europe.

Because I stretched every penny, I wasn't used to drinking--and the little I had done this evening had helped to intensify my mood. I felt I couldn't relax too much because I lacked the cash, while the unaccustomed alcohol and gaiety made me feel more like an outsider.

Several hours later, as I left the club with a slight stagger, I had made up my mind that it was now time for the great adventure. Boyish notions of romantic hardship, danger, and *"beau geste"* distorted my thoughts. Hitchhiking was kid stuff. I wanted stronger meat.

"Have a good night, Ronnie, and I will see you in the morning," Kurt said with a warm smile.

"Thanks, Kurt, you can see me to my train to Paris tomorrow."

"But I thought you would visit with me for a few weeks."

"Sorry, my friend, but tomorrow I move on."

Before going to bed and sleep, I took inventory of my finances. I had saved practically every cent I earned on the Norwegian ship in the few months we plied the waters in the area of the midnight sun. The savings totaled about fourteen hundred kroner, or slightly more than three hundred dollars American. These savings were carried in my grouch bag, which the second cook aboard ship had shown me how to make. This belt later was to figure in my escaping from the Foreign Legion.

CHAPTER 2

Throughout the night I tossed and turned, wrestling with my decision to join the Legion. It was my belief that I could try anything once, and that this would be the ultimate adventure of my life. As far back as I could remember, the romantic and adventurous exploits of soldiers of fortune had intrigued me. Distant places held an enchantment. A year after my first attempt to see the world had taken me to Washington, D.C., I went on a hitchhiking jaunt to Chicago, which ended with my being placed in a detention home until my folks came after me.

After my junior year in high school, I hit the open road again. My craving for unusual experiences led me to join up with a carnival in Kansas. Life with the carnies was educational, and I learned the ropes working the hanky-panks or minor games of chance, and observing the wild parties of the carnies after work.

Then I had wandered to California and to northern Nevada, where I became a ranch hand near a town called Winnemucca. My wanderlust also found me paddling a canoe down the Allegheny River in the hope of reaching New Orleans via the Ohio and Mississippi rivers. But this trip was scuttled in a few days when the canoe was swamped in rapids.

Then it was back to California, where I finally got a job on a pear ranch after waiting around for five days. I had to sleep all night in front of the hiring gate to be sure of being among the two hundred picked for work. I worked as a swamper, whose job it was to carry boxes of fruit from the orchards to the warehouse.

My wanderings took me through many states and into Mexico, where I visited the Aztec Ruins. Before scraping up enough for a one-way ticket to Europe, I worked as a cabana boy and lifeguard at a Miami Beach resort. When I finally had enough for a boat ticket, I flipped a coin to see whether I should go to Alaska or Europe. Europe won out.

The morning sunshine chased away the blues. I relaxed because of my decision to join *la Légion étrangère*. I felt the question was now out of my hands. The die was cast. Premonitions of a rough life in the Legion gave me momentary qualms, but I wanted to best any challenge.

I got up, threw some water on my face, ran a comb through my hair and jumped into a pair of slacks and a T-shirt. There still were a few hours to kill before meeting Kurt for lunch, so I took in the sights of West Berlin. They reminded me of sections of good old New York City.

At noon I walked into Kurt's newspaper office. The receptionist picked up an interphone and asked for display advertising. She no sooner hung up then Kurt was bounding down the stairs toward me.

"Ronnie, tell me you have decided not to leave us."

"Sorry, Kurt, but my mind is made up. I get the next train for Paris within two hours."

"Isn't there anything I can do keep you here awhile?"

I shook my head. We walked out of the office and strolled for a half hour.

"Well, old friend, this is it for a while," I said. "I'll write to you."

"I'll miss you, Ronnie. Please take care, and may God bless you." were Kurt's parting remarks.

I went back to the hostel and found that Kurt already had taken care of the tab. I packed all my possessions in a small gym bag and went to the Zoo station. This would be the first time in months that I took a train. I usually auto-stopped or hitchhiked.

It required a special visa to get through East Germany. The Russian authorities were a somber lot but the visa proved easy to obtain.

The trip to Paris took about twenty-four hours. A hunk of cheese and some bread that I had packed in the ditty bag came in handy. The ancient train pulled into the Gare du Nord station in the northern end of Paris late in the afternoon. I managed to find a comparatively cheap hotel, the Place du Don. The skinny looking clerk peered over his glasses, signed me in and pointed to the stairway. My key number was 503, which meant hiking up five flights.

The cheaply furnished room contained an iron coaster bed, a bureau with a mirror, a pitcher and a bowl. A bare light bulb was suspended from the high ceiling. The only window overlooked a courtyard. There was no balcony and no fire escape. I tossed my bag on a chair, refreshed myself, and went out for some bread, cheese, and a quart of milk. I brought the food back to the hotel, and sat munching it with my feet propped up at the open window.

In the morning I found a gendarme and asked him to direct me to the enlistment office for the Legion, which was far out from the center of Paris at Fort de Vincennes. The metro took me underground and within a short time I was talking to a few French regulars guarding the front gate.

"What brings an American here?" asked one of the soldiers.

"I'd like to join your Legion," I told him. The trio seemed to have a private joke of their own, and after much chuckling and untranslatable phrases in French, I was led to the rear of the fort to an office where I met my first Legionnaire. He was a brutal looking sergeant of German extraction, with sun bronzed skin, and sharp features.

"So you wish to join us," he snapped.

"That's why I'm here," I replied in my best military voice, which wasn't too impressive. My previous time in uniform had been limited to a couple of months in a military school.

"Let me see your passport," he growled.

I hardly expected the sergeant to look pleased, but I was a bit taken aback when he snatched the passport, glanced at it, then threw it into a drawer. He summoned a sous-officier of corporal rank to escort me to another office upstairs. Before leaving, the sergeant asked me why I wanted to join the Legion.

"For adventure." I answered. The sergeant grunted and waved to the corporal, and away we went.

I was led to a barren office and sat in a straight-backed wooden chair. A few others were waiting to be interviewed by the officer. Seated next to me was a Belgian around forty-five. He was neatly attired and looked very sad. He spoke broken English and managed to convey to me that he was joining to get away from a nagging wife. A look around the room disclosed a derelict wino, an obviously hardened criminal, and a dapper looking sharpie who could easily pass as a gigolo.

The corporal explained the requirements, which were not too stringent. First, your age had to be between eighteen and forty, and secondly, you had to pass the physical. The sous-officier motioned to me and I was taken to an inner office. The corporal closed the door on his way out and left me facing a handsome French captain who looked smart in his uniform with three rows of decorations. The officer startled me with his impeccable English.

"And what is the reason for such a young Yankee to come to the Legion?"

"As I answered before to your sergeant, sir, it is strictly for adventure."

"Are you sure you know what you are doing?" he asked.

"I'm fully aware what's in store for me, sir."

"I don't think you are. First of all, let me warn you that Legion life is very difficult. The discipline is strict, living conditions are not what an American is accustomed to; life in the desert is almost unbearable with day to day details and operations in the mountains. Do you think you can put up with this routine for five years?"

I figured the captain was using a negative approach, and I was determined that nothing would change my mind.

"That's why I'm here Captain," I answered firmly.

"Very well, Monsieur Reynolds, you have twenty-four hours in which to make your final decision. I shall expect to see you Monday morning at this time. Until then, *bonjour.*"

The corporal led me to the gate, and as I walked toward the city he said, "Think it over, Johnny." I was soon to find out that any Yank or Englishman in the Legion was referred to as Johnny. Since this was Saturday, I actually had forty-eight hours in which to make up my mind.

The weekend just delayed things and gave me more time for reminiscing, which wasn't always pleasant. My earlier life had not been unhappy. In fact, the problem was that it was just the opposite. As I thought of my family back in Buffalo, I knew that they would not approve. My parents had some tough breaks during the Depression, and also during the war when my father entered the service. Now in their middle years, life was easier -- except that they were cursed with a wandering son. Thoughts of my sister and of not seeing her for five years were not conducive to gaiety either.

Sunday in Paris in September may be romantic for some people, but it passed me by. There was the Eiffel Tower in the background, and there I was, a future tough Legionnaire, nibbling cookies as I walked and stared at the nurses pushing baby buggies. My courage wasn't enough to promote anything here. I fingered my pocket and realized my passport was missing. It was still in the drawer in the recruiting office. Sunday night I lay in bed in the cheap walk-up hotel and attempted to examine my conscience. In a few hours I would be signing away five years of my life to become a mercenary. It seemed like only last week that I arrived in England. In the six months I was over there I had really taken in the sights. With only fifty dollars to my name, I hitchhiked throughout England, Wales, Ireland, and Scotland. I was able to live on one dollar a day. My nights were spent mostly in the youth hostels set up throughout Europe for the use of traveling young people.

I suppose I always had a secret desire to become a soldier of fortune, ever since childhood. What probably encouraged my thinking along those lines was my acquaintance with a dishwasher named Ensio Tiira. He was a Finn who worked with me in the basement caverns of the Grand Hotel in Stockholm. He had served in the Foreign Legion, and had deserted and written a popular book, *"Raft of Despair,"* about his escape and experiences on a raft. He had spent his proceeds from the book and again was wandering about Europe.

I tossed upon the old-fashioned bed and realized I could still change my mind. Then I recalled one of my last letters home from aboard the Appian. It was then I realized my subconscious definitely had no intention of settling down.

I remembered my last letter home. It read in part...

> *"I don't think I'll be home for a while, Mom and Dad. I really miss you very much, but feel I must look around while I have the opportunity. And besides, I want to prove once and for all that with the means God equipped me with, I can strike out and successfully fend for myself."*

I knew then what I had to do the next morning.

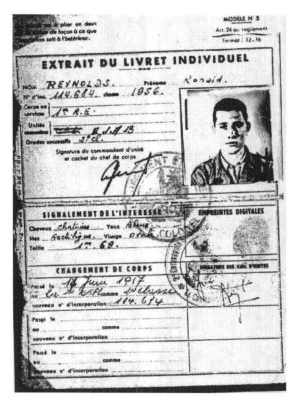

This identification card is a grim reminder of Reynold's
18 months of misery in the Legion of Lost Souls.

CHAPTER 3

The morning seemed to come exceptionally fast. My watch showed 7:25 and the sun already was peeking into the courtyard below. I slipped into a pair of slacks and a sports jacket over my t-shirt, pushed on my comfortable leather boots shipped to me in Norway by the folks, and used the community type bathroom at the end of the hall. The rest of my meager possessions I tossed into my small carrying case and hiked down the five flights of stairs to the room clerk's cage to settle up my bill.

"Will Monsieur be checking in with us again in the near future?"

"*Mon ami,* my next billet assignment will be quite lengthy, but until we meet again, bonjour."

This day, September 10, 1956, was just five months since my departure from home. As the subway edged its way to the outskirts of Paris and the old fort, I wondered how many more months it would be before I saw my loved ones again.

I got off the cars near the two-story castle type structure of black stone. The fort went back to medieval days. The moat ringing the buttress was overrun with weeds and stones. The weather beaten drawbridge was lowered, and from all appearances, hadn't been raised in over half a century. I halted in my tracks, taking in the depressing prison-like sight. Narrow windows and parapets were numerous. At the gate of Fort De Vincennes two French regular soldiers stood guard.

"I was here Saturday and was told to return if I still wanted to enlist," I told the guard.

"Through that door and up one flight of stairs to the first office on your right."

The weather-beaten sergeant was sitting behind a desk with a cigarette dangling from the side of his mouth. He peered at me through the smokescreen he had set up, and without taking the cigarette from between his lips, snarled, "Oh-ho, Johnny, I did not expect to see you again."

"My mind's made up sergeant. Where do I go from here?"

"Patience. Patience. You will have plenty of time with us. No need to rush things," he smirked. The burly sous-officier reached into a manila folder, grabbed a few papers, and led me to a room with another non-com. I signed more papers and was then interviewed by a lieutenant. The usual questions ensued. My name, where did I live, why did I want to join the Legion, and so on. There were still more signatures, and I swear I'll never know which one actually committed me and made me an official member of *1A Légion étrangère.*

This routine was becoming wearisome, and finally I was returned to the office of the good looking captain of Saturday. The interrogators had gone up in rank step by step. The captain's office was bare, except for his desk. He seemed to look through me from behind his dark glasses and said, "I hope you have thought over well my advice to you."

"Yes, captain, and I still wish to become a Legionnaire."

"To be frank with you, Reynolds, we do not like to take Americans into the Legion. You Yanks are the type that rebel against our kind of life. You chaps have a record of not getting along in the Legion."

"I assure you, sir, that I'm most anxious to join the Legion for the reasons I gave you the other day."

The captain rubbed his chin, then typed a few notes. My interview had lasted about ten minutes. I was beginning to get restless and scraped my feet on the bare stone floor.

The captain looked up and said in a firm but pleasant voice, "Very well Legionnaire Reynolds. Return to the office of the sergeant and hand him this portfolio." As I was leaving he called out, "Good luck."

I wondered what it was he was trying to see in me. Several months later, while reading an issue of the Legion magazine, *Képi Blanc,* I found out that this captain was blind. He had lost his eyesight in Legion conflict and was given the post at Fort De Vincennes as an honor. The lean six footer was a real pro. It wasn't hard to comprehend that he had earned the Legion of Honor.

The captain had not offered to shake hands. The camaraderie of soldiers didn't go this far between a new private and a veteran captain. I got the impression that all recruits didn't get to see the captain. Also, I felt that the Legion officers were surprised and curious as to why a Yank would give up the wealth of America for the hardships of the Legion. Along with some other recruits, I went through a physical. This was not rigid, but a few failed. One of those rejected was an alcoholic and another had tuberculosis.

My life in the Legion began shortly after I closed the big door leading from the captain's office, because from then on everything was, *"Vite, Vite, Vite!* On the double! Hurry! Hurry!" When I came face to face with my friend, La sergeant, I knew damned well that I was now a full-fledged member of the French Foreign Legion.

"OK, *Monsieur Private,"* he growled. Into the next room and off with all of your clothes."

I was pushed into a storeroom to change. I took off my civvies. The corduroy sports jacket which had been given me by a cook aboard the Appian came off, along with my khaki pants. My clothes were taken by a Legionnaire in attendance, wrapped into the sports jacket and folded into a knot by the sleeves. Another of the men working in the stores indicated in broken English that I wouldn't be able to keep my comfortable boots. He conned me into giving them to him. That probably was one of the worst decisions I ever made, aside from joining up in the first place. I learned later that I could have kept my boots. And for the duration of my time in the Legion, I suffered constantly from foot trouble because of the ill-fitting second-hand footwear issued. The routants were high-styled, and either too tight or too loose. During my days in uniform I made several exchanges, but never came close to a comfortable fit. My uniform at this time was a pair of coveralls, a kelly overseas cap, the abominable work shoes, and a small supply of underwear and socks. My bundle of clothes and private possessions were tagged with my name and shipped to Africa. I saw them weeks later at Sidi Bel-Abbès, the Legion capital. We were supposed to be paid for the clothing at that time, but I was talked into donating most of it for the needy town folks. These people must have been really needy if they were worse off than the Legionnaires. The amount of cash I could have obtained wasn't worth fighting about. The N.C.O.'s evidently had a racket going by selling civilian clothing. The clothing issue at the storeroom was supplemented with a bar of strong yellow soap, a toothbrush, a fork and spoon, a canteen and cup. I had my own shaving gear. My hair was clipped short. When the so-called barber was done, I realized why no comb had been issued. I was led to my quarters. This was a large dormitory, bare except for a few dozen bunk beds. The ceilings were high and one bare light bulb hung in the center. There were few windows, and they were high. The bunk beds were made of steel, and had straw mattresses. A mattress cover was not issued at the fort, but later on we received a rubberized mattress cover which was exchanged every two months. Legionnaires did not have a surplus of personal goods, as there was no place to keep them. There were no foot lockers or clothing cabinets.

There were only three other recruits in the dormitory when I wandered in, and all seemed lost in thought. I grabbed the bunk along the wall, and had my meager personal effects stashed away when a corporal came up to me and bellowed in a combination of French and German. I didn't understand the words, but the bucket of water and brush made clear what he had in mind. The rookies were the obvious clean up men. When we weren't scrubbing the floor, we emptied slop buckets. It didn't take long to master the brush and water, and to follow through with a drying rag, but I sure would have welcomed a mop. When a job was finished I would wander back to the near empty dormitory. Soon a sous-officier would appear and rattle off in French.

After we scrubbed the dormitory, we did the same to the larger hall and the sous-officiers canteen. The other rookies and I were becoming bewildered, and we were wondering how long we had to do these menial tasks, since we had joined to be soldiers. I had arrived at Fort De Vincennes a day too late. A group of more than two hundred had just left. There were only a couple of other bleus, or greenhorns at the fort. And it appeared that we would be here for days until a new complement was made up for shipment to Marseilles.

My fellow recruits included a Spaniard named Francesco and a German by the name of Hans. Neither was too friendly. We spoke very little, because of the language barrier, but there were a few times we were able to make ourselves understood with hand signals and expressions.

A corporal walked into the dormitory and yelled, *"Soupe! Soupe! Alors!"* I figured *'Soupe'* was soup, and I wasn't far off. It meant chow. The three of us followed the sous-officier to the mess hall, where we joined a dozen or so regular Legionnaires stationed at the fort. Legionnaires were responding to the call of Soupe on the double, running into the mess hall with their canteens, cups, and spoons. I walked up to a table that was empty and was joined by the two other recruits. Four veteran Legionnaires also seated themselves at our table and began pounding their forks on the glass plates. *"Apportez moi un potage!"* yelled one of the dirty looking *anciens,* or old timers. The soldier assigned to KP duty walked out of the kitchen with a big bucket and began scooping out its contents onto the dishes. My first meal in the Legion was to be one repeated daily for my entire enlistment. It consisted of lentils, potatoes, and gravy with strings of what appeared to be the remnants of camel or horse meat. I never was to have real meat served to me in a Legion mess hall.

Another kitchen helper moved up and down the tables with a large sprinkling can. It contained a red wine, and I nearly choked on it. Even though it tasted like strong vinegar, the *pinard* still had a high alcoholic content. I was chewing the beans and washing them down with the pinard, when I gave out a yelp.

"S'avez-vous?" asked one Legionnaire.

"My tooth, my tooth," I cried. "I broke my tooth on a stone." The anciens thought this hilarious, and gave out with hearty guffaws. I managed to finish the meal; I was hungry. The only food we had plenty of was bread. Without a doubt, bread was the staff of life to a Legion meal. It came in big round loaves, and each of us got a quarter of the thick loaf. It wasn't too bad, and it was filling. Butter would have been ideal, but we never would see that luxury in the Legion. We did get coffee.

"Sugar and cream someone, please." I muttered. One of the anciens eyed me with contempt.

"Bleu, you drink coffee black. No sugar. *Café au lait,* you get on Sunday."

I returned to the dormitory feeling miserable from the broken tooth and the slop and the wine. I knew I couldn't get out of the fort on pass. We were informed that our first liberty would come in five months. I lay down on my bunk and must have stared at the ceiling for about two hours when a loud whistle blast jerked me to a sitting position. A sergeant had walked in and given the customary lights out signal. It was ten PM. I was tired, but couldn't go right to sleep. I wondered what I had gotten myself into. Would this continue? Was this what the Legion was really like? It had to get better. The Legion couldn't be composed of scrub women. I was tired and confused. Soldiering just couldn't be a long succession of menial details. I got some peace by saying my prayers. It seemed too conspicuous to kneel at the side of the bunk. No one else did.

Again I asked myself why had I really joined? Familiar responses came to mind. I was restless and curious; this would be the epitome of experience. All of my traveling and jobs had jaded me; wandering over the U.S. had become dull, and Europe was somewhat of a disappointment. The novelty and adventure of traveling had worn off. While I had been standing watch for many long, dreary hours on the Norwegian ship, my mind had plenty of time to revolve, and it kept coming up with: join the Foreign Legion. Thoughts of death in the Legion had appeared, but only in a vague and romantic way. I was too young to take death seriously. These thoughts ran through my mind as I slowly fell off to sleep following my first full day as a member of the famed French Foreign Legion.

CHAPTER 4

The bell came as a rude awakening with the sergeant
entering at six AM and letting loose with several piercing
blasts of his whistle.

"Allons la haut tout le monde et faire le lit!" He
bellowed. Without a doubt he was telling us to hit the
deck and make up our sacks.

I got up reluctantly. There wasn't much to making
up the bed, the blanket was folded at the foot of the
bunk. My few clothes were stashed in two square
bundles on the flat steel rack over the bed. The piling
of one's clothing in neat squares is known as *paquetage*.
I was to learn later that if the two bundles didn't form

a perfect square at right angles, the inspecting officer would send the whole array crashing to the floor.

Next came, *"l'appel."* It seemed ridiculous to have a roll call for only three men. My day in the Legion was falling into a routine. I found my way to and from the washroom and joined Francesco and Hans in the mess hall. Breakfast was just as much a shock as evening chow. We were each given a hunk of bread, and a can of sardines was tossed on the table to be split up among the three of us. Then there was coffee without milk. When I went to reach for my four measly pieces of fish, the can was empty. Hans had taken my share. I figured this was as good a time as any to have an understanding.

"OK, kraut-head, get wise." I shouted, as my fork stabbed five of the eight sardines in Han's dish. Before the startled German could come to his senses, I unsheathed my hunting knife and placed it next to my plate. The anciens laughed vulgarly at the German's retreat and Hans eyed me with hatred, but said and did nothing.

The rest of the morning was taken up with work details which consisted of mopping operations. Shortly before lunch, I went into the chamber and found several new recruits. Francesco was strutting around like the undisputed king of the mountain, practically daring anyone to challenge his reign. He was a perfect type for a dead end kid roll, sinewy, wiry, strong and belligerent. The new batch of bleus tried to ignore him, but Cisco wouldn't be shut aside. He took a fire axe from the wall, made with Indian war whoops, and imbedded it several inches into the floor. I guess he figured he had shown the bunch how tough he was, but all he had accomplished was to make himself as popular as a polecat.

I was getting my utensils when someone yelled, "Hey Johnny, out of that bunk. I picked it for myself!"

I looked up with a start but found no one trying to take over my sack. Then in the far end of the chamber, Hans strode belligerently toward a big, good looking, curly headed blond. When the blond answered in almost flawless English, I realized why he was called Johnny.

"I did not know these bunks were reserved. I suggest you get yourself another one." Hans became even more enraged at the laughter from the rest of the Legionnaires. "Swine!" screamed Hans. He never did get to finish his tirade for the big blond's fist shot out like a bullet and connected with Han's jaw, sending the German crumbling to the floor.

At that moment a sergeant came upon the scene and the gibbering Hans appealed to him, *"Ich fordere Ihren schutz. Dieser mensch hat mich beleidgt."*

"What's he stammering about?" I asked the blond.

"He's asking the sous-officier for protection," he replied. "Claims I insulted him."

The sergeant was more annoyed with Hans than the blond, and said with disgust, *"Feigling. Lache.* Coward." He stormed from the chamber and Hans sulked back to his bunk.

"Nice going, fella," I said. "Who are you?"

"My name is Eric, What's yours?"

"Mine is Ron. I'm an American. Are you English?"

"Oh no, Norwegian. My home is outside of Oslo." From that moment on, Eric and I had a lot in common. We both spoke English, and I was acquainted with his country, having sailed out of Norway on the Appian.

The rest of the week was along the same routine of meager meals and *corveés,* or work details. In addition to the deck swabbing, I had to help finish off an officer's recreation room called the *"pouput."* There was no rec room for privates.

The old fort was beginning to fill up, and I figured soon we would be shipped off to Marseilles for preliminary training. In spite of more people around, I was living within myself. I was wondering if I had done the right thing, since most of the men didn't speak English.

After a week it was time to ship out. There were now about twenty of us, including a red-headed Belgian and two husky beef-faced Irishmen. For traveling we were issued second-hand Legion uniforms of wool. They were much like an American G. I. outfit, complete with an Eisenhower type jacket. It would be months before we could earn the right to wear the famed Legion kepi. We were ordered to pack our gear and line up. Next came l'appel.

"Rassemblement, couvrez sur deux," barked the sergeant. *"En avant,"* and we marched out of the fort to a truck, which carted us to the station. It was the first time I had left the fort since enlisting.

On the train we were segregated from the civilians, and cramped three to a seat. On the thirty-six hour train ride my seat mates identified themselves as Dominic from Salerno, Italy, and Werner from Bremen, Germany. Both of them spoke a little English.

"What are you doing here Dominic?" I inquired.

"I am not in good graces of the Carabiniere in my country."

"Are you wanted for a crime?"

"Let us say they would be happy to see me in prison." Then Dominic explained that one day while driving his motorcycle through a school zone a youngster ran out into his path and was killed. Dominic panicked and fled. Learning that he was being sought on homicide charges, he fled the country, got to Paris, and signed up.

"What about you, Johnny?" he asked me.

"Nobody seems to believe me, but I really joined for adventure. To tell you the truth, if this past week is any example of typical Legion life, I want out."

Werner jabbed Dominic in the ribs, looked over at me and started to laugh.

"What's so funny?" I asked.

"You joined for adventure. Ha, you will get more than you bargained for."

"What do you know about Legion life?" I snapped back.

"Ha, Ha. You are a bleu. I already served five years with la Légion étrangère. I am reenlisting. You are just a -- how do you say in your country? -- a greenhorn."

Dominic chimed in, "If you are lucky enough to survive your enlistment you can rejoin and get a bonus of thirty-five thousand francs, which is about one hundred dollars American."

"Speaking of money," I asked, "What's the pay in this outfit?"

Dominic volunteered the answer. "During the instruction period you will get about three dollars a month." This revelation only firmed up my belief that what I was doing was ridiculous. It was getting dark now, and I munched on a biscuit from my rations. The train lulled me to sleep.

The sunlight, magnified by the train window, burned into my face and woke me up. Dominic and Werner already had awakened and were cramped in the corner of the coach playing cards with a couple of other recruits. I stretched my legs, swayed to the commode, freshened up a bit, and munched more of my K-rations.

I longed to see some of the civilian passengers, and started to make my way out of the Legion coach when an armed guard stepped out of the shadows and blocked my way.

"Back up with the rest of the swine" yelled the towering German sergeant.

I shuffled back to my seat next to the window and stared out at the scenery. As our train got closer to southern France, the landscape took on a different view. The hillsides were covered with vineyards and the air seemed dustier. I spent the rest of the day reading *"Moulin Rouge"* and catching forty winks now and then.

The sun was sinking fast now, and the three of us took up our positions for the night. At sunup our destination was about reached. Soon, beautiful Marseilles Bay was in sight. The train slowed and as it began to screech to a halt, a sous-officier appeared at the head of the car and shouted, *"Faites grande sacs -- tout Le monde en bas."*

"That means to make up your packs and turn out, Johnny," Dominic confirmed.

As we stepped into the bright sunlight, we were lined up for roll call. Three sous-officiers from the fort stepped forward and herded us into trucks for the trip up the mountain to the ancient stronghold. We really got a fast shuffle from the depot. I couldn't even pick up a candy bar or magazine, much less talk to any civilian. Our contingent of twenty men was ordered aboard a troop carrier truck. The rumbling trucks finally came to a halt, and we were lined up once again, this time at the gates of Fort Nicholas. It was a picture to behold. The ancient fort was a smooth, yellow, stucco, castle-like structure with dozens of parapets, and was peaked with a gold madonna statue. Surrounded on three sides by sheer cliffs, which dropped to jagged boulders along the banks of the Mediterranean some fifty feet below, The fort needed no moat. Several small buildings made up the rest of the site. The roofs were of red tile, the same as most houses in Europe. I was beat, disheveled, and disgusted at this stage, and really couldn't appreciate the beauty surrounding me. Even the sight of girls in bikinis sunbathing on the beaches nearby failed to arouse much interest in me. This only made me realize that I had not made a very smart move when I enlisted.

Bivuac made with trucks at mountain as men await copters to take them as close as possible to rebel areas. They travel light because they will have to march for days in the mountains.

CHAPTER 5

The first day at the fort was rough. We spent hours getting processed. We were shuffled from one bureau to another, signed a slew of papers, repeated a multitude of answers to interpreters, were in and out of long lines -- and all in temperatures over one hundred degrees.

About the time I was ready to drop from exhaustion, we were marched into our bed chamber, and I made for the nearest bunk and plopped down, clothes and all. I must have dozed for a half hour before I was rudely awakened by a boot in the face. It was my bunk mate climbing into the upper sack.

"Sorry, Johnny, clumsy of me."

"That's OK, fellow. The name is Ron, what's yours?"

"I am Carlos from Portuguese, South Africa. And there began the one true friendship I was to develop in the Legion.

"Where do you come from, Ron?"

"From New York State, the city of Buffalo on Lake Erie to be exact."

"I have always wanted to visit your country, but most of my traveling has been only in the jungles of Africa."

I learned that Carlos was a true adventurer. He was in his early thirties, only about five feet seven inches tall, but built like an Adonis. He was to become the strongest man in our outfit. As we lay in our bunks briefing one another on our past, I learned that Carlos had left Mozambique with his goal set for the French Foreign Legion. Traveling light, he started up through the wilds of Africa in a canoe. He spent months in the jungle, stopping off in native villages, and sometimes living it up like a white God. Some native tribes figured him for a missionary and gave him the red carpet treatment. He would be given a hut, fed, clothed, and provided with a woman companion, usually a daughter of the native chief. When the situation became too delicate, Carlos would take off in the middle of the night and paddle to another village. His luck finally ran out when his canoe was swamped and lost in rapids. He made it to shore and walked the rest of the way to French Equatorial Africa, where he arrived at a Legion fort, and was then sent on by the Legion. Prior to this hazardous journey,

Carlos led a playboy life, in a rugged sort of way. He spent six months at a time hunting crocodiles in the jungles. He would hunt by night from a flatboat on the uncharted, foul-smelling rivers, armed only with a light and a spear. Carlos, a nonconformist, lightened the tedium by taking along a companion-- a blonde, bosomy show girl named Tina.

"You know, Ron, there is an art to hunting crocs. You must harpoon them and get them between the eyes, then tow their carcasses to shore. If you didn't use a spear with a line, the beasts would sink to the bottom and never come to the surface." Now he was giving all of this up because of his desire to become a soldier of fortune.

I gave Carlos a breakdown on my home life, and my many excursions throughout the United States and Europe.

"Your sister, Sue, Ron -- is she as pretty as you are handsome?"

"None of your blarney, Carlos. See for yourself. Here is a picture of my sister and parents."

'I la voulez, oui,' I thought. "She is *trés chic*. Someday I will write to her."

A sous-officier appeared and bellowed, "Soupe!" We followed the stampeding recruits to the mess hall. Here the chow was just as miserable as at Paris, consisting of beans, bread, potatoes, and stringy gravy. The only gratifying part of the meal was the liter of pinard.

Probably the most shocking condition in all Legion forts was the French latrine, and the one at Fort Nicholas was no exception. The bathroom was a large chamber with individual stalls. There was no commode, only a hole in the floor, in front of which were two depressions in the shape of feet. The waste overflowed from the top of the filled tanks onto the floor. Hundreds of flies and other insects helped shorten your visit. I realized that I had taken for granted the seemingly insignificant conveniences at home. Once a week we got a shower, and we never had hot water. The deplorable conditions of the latrine weren't much worse than our sleeping arrangements. I was considered lucky because my bunk bed was one of the few that wasn't infested with *poinez,* or thumb tacks.

That first night at Fort Nicholas was terrible for ninety percent of the recruits. After much cursing and yelling, the majority of the men left their mattresses and carried their blankets outside. Even that didn't help since the ticks and bedbugs managed to secret themselves in the clothing of the restless Legionnaires. The night of torment was evidenced the next day when the Legionnaires shed their shirts in the courtyard for a bit of sun during their short siestas. Their backs and arms were covered with red bites from the pests.

My first work detail was a nauseous assignment -- garbage. We were marched to a huge bin and ordered to shove the mountainous mess into open trucks for hauling to the dumps. The huge piles had come alive under the scorching sun, and the putrid odor was almost unbearable. When the trucks were loaded we rode them out of the fort. We were dressed in crawling coveralls on board a stinking garbage truck rolling along the coast of the Riviera, the playground of the world. This was the Cote d'Azur. I could look at it, like Moses near the Promised Land, but that was as close as I could get. The road clung tightly to the coast and I could look down on bathers wearing little but a suntan. While unloading the sickening contents of the trucks into the rodent-infested dumps my mind was becoming heavy with the thought of the beautiful Riviera. The trip back convinced me that I had made a foolish decision at the Legion.

That night, three hours after lights out, the roar of a sergeant brought us to our feet for l'appel.

"What's the roll call for Carlos?" I asked my bunkmate.

"It seems that some of our chickens have flown the coop," replied Carlos.

Tied from a nearby window were several rubber sheets. Three Spaniards had lowered themselves and dropped to the jagged rocks below. Their heroic efforts weren't successful. Foolishly, they had walked along the road in their Legion fatigues and were spotted. The Spaniards were unaware of the seriousness of their crime, but soon we were all given the lesson. The escapees were taken outdoors and all of the recruits were ordered to observe the proceedings. The captain explained the duties of a Legionnaire and the punishment meted out for those who failed to live up to the rigors of Legion life. Then, as an example for those disillusioned recruits who also might have any ideas of escaping, the trio was flogged by a huge corporal until they were unable to stand. Then they were hauled off to the *tole,* or regimental prison.

It was difficult getting back to sleep that night. It was a strain to remember if I had ever been a civilian. All I could see behind my tightly shut eyes was the bloody beating administered to the captured escapees. Even with that horrid picture before me, I began to make plans to escape. My mind was in a turmoil between the desire to flee, and the lesson of what would happen if I were caught.

The next day I was assigned to the best of details. I was sent to a *poubliez,* or convalescent home for Legionnaires, just north of Marseilles. It was a pitiful sight. These were maimed soldiers of fortune who chose to stay in the Legion rather than be a burden to their families back home. The fallen warriors displayed empty sleeves and pant legs, and some were blind. Many were veterans of the Indo-China campaign. They were kept active doing farm work and working on metal and leather crafts. The paltry sums they collected for their finished products were used to keep them in drink.

The poubliez was one of the most modern structures in the entire Legion. It had the appearance of a good motel, and was the opposite of Legion life in the fort. Two patients shared a neat room. The men here were still Legionnaires, although they could be discharged if they desired. For the first time in their Legion career, they were treated like human beings. The chow was good and it was the first time I saw meat while in the Legion.

My job was to help construct new buildings. I thought that this would be a good place for me if I were maimed, rather than go home in that condition. Some men wounded themselves to get out of the Legion, or frequently committed suicide. You could not shoot yourself and wind up in the poubliez, though. The Legion wanted its five years' service out of you, and if you could work at all, you finished your term, even if you were minus a leg or arm. Then you would be eligible for the poubliez, but not if the wound was self-inflicted. I then learned that one of the papers I had signed when enlisting released the French from any claim for any wounds or sickness of any kind.

One of the oldest Legionnaires at the convalescent camp was an Italian by the name of Mariano, who was one of the handful of survivors when the Germans broke through the Maginot Line on May 10, 1940. Missing an arm and a leg, Mariano spent his working days weaving baskets with one hand. Still in a state of semi-shock, he vividly recalled how a few thousand Legionaries held off the German army for forty-eight hours to permit the

French force to, find safe positions. He was one of the few to make it back to Sidi Bel Abbes.

My next detail was KP. About twenty of us spent hours peeling rotten potatoes and carrots. Peeling potatoes is a classic army joke, but it wasn't funny to me because all I could think of was how hungry I was. When the sergeants assigned to watch over us weren't looking my way, I would eat a potato or carrot. If I were lucky, I would be able to hide a couple in my pockets. Hunger was becoming a hardship, and I was to find it prevalent throughout the Legion. A sought after detail was cleaning the officers mess. The officers ate well and the Legionnaires assigned to their mess had a chance to eat the scraps left on their plates. For many of the Legionnaires, this was their only opportunity to taste scraps of meat.

We became less civilized as the hunger grew. There was constant arguing at meals, and snarling over every scrap. We began to act like hungry dogs, rather than men. One man would serve for each table. Usually he favored his friends. This naturally caused a lot of dissension. There was never enough to go around, especially the gravy with its faint hint of meat. When Hans, the surly German, had the turn of ladling out the food, I wound up hungrier than usual. I noticed that Francesco tried to favor me a bit. I was so hungry and also so grateful for any kind word, that Francesco and I soon began talking in the barracks at night-- although we had to converse in halting English and Spanish. Francesco was short and dark with a slight droop in one eyelid. The eye made him look rather stupid, but actually he was quite perceptive. The usual question came up, "Why did you join?"

"Adventure," I answered. By now this was beginning to sound silly, even to me.

"Is there no chance for adventure in America? I ran out of adventure in my country. How about you?"

"I join up for job for five years, and get fed." "We both got gypped," I laughed.

There was a group of Spaniards a few bunks away who got on my nerves with their constant chattering. Their words seemed to come out in staccato bursts. Their energy and liveliness sometimes tired me. Frequently they would join in melancholy songs. This affected their listeners more than themselves. When not singing they argued, very heatedly. And I swore they were about to pull out their knives at times. Gradually I realized that they were not going to cut each other. My original dislike slowly changed as time went on. The Spanish made some of the best buddies. One reason for my original feelings was that these Spaniards reminded me of the South American who had conned me out of my boots. Whenever my feet hurt I cursed the whole Latin race.

CHAPTER 6

Time was drawing near for our leaving *"La Belle France."* If the treatment we had thus far was any indication, I didn't relish what was in store for me in the months ahead on regular Legion duty. Neither did Nicholas, a Greek God from Athens, who bunked nearby. It was time for the grand l'appel, the last night in Marseilles, when Nick went berserk.

The corporal was bed-checking when Nick leaped from his upper bunk and grabbed him by the neck. The rest of us stood by motionless, frozen in disbelief, as Nicholas picked up the sous-officier and smashed him repeatedly against the wall. Screaming epithets in Greek, Nick kept up the battering until a sergeant-chef burst into the room and felled him with the butt of his rifle. The corporal was carried to the dispensary, while the Greek was dragged to his feet and hauled into the courtyard. The entire complement of recruits was assembled for the so-called trial of the rebellious Legionnaire.

Several officers and sous-officiers participated. Nick was pummeled with fists, clubbed with rifles, and lashed with a whip while we stood by helplessly. His bloody body was then dragged away, presumably to the brig for the night, to await transportation to Colomb Béchar, the Legion penal camp in Algeria near the Moroccan border. None of us ever saw or heard from Nick again. Rumor had it that he was shot to death while he was trying to escape from the dreaded prison. Nick's treatment really struck home, his punishment served as a warning.

The next morning, we made preparation for shipping to Oran, Algeria by troop ship. However, before we lined up outside the fort for a final muster and boarding of trucks, we were given another going over by still another agency.

"Hey, Carlos, why are those black vans pulling into the courtyard?"

"Those vans, ami, are similar to the black Maria's in your country that are used to transport prisoners to the jail. Those men are members of the *Deuxieme Bureau,* or the secret police. Something like your FBI."

"What are they doing here? Who are they looking for?"

"You need not worry Ronnie. They are seeking wanted men from various countries who are traced through the Interpol."

They finally got around to me and really gave me the third degree.

"What is your real name? Where are you from? Why did you come into the Legion? What are you running away from? Were you in any trouble in the United States? Does your embassy know where you are?" These and dozens of other questions were fired at me in machine gun fashion for almost two hours before the chief interrogator threw up his hands and finished with me. I didn't know who they were looking for, but it sure took a lot of convincing to prove that I was just plain Ron Reynolds, a would be soldier of fortune who actually was in this mess solely for so-called adventure. In the old days anyone could find asylum and immunity in the Legion. This is not the case now, but a few do manage to slip in and fool the police. An old timer told me, "If you get by Marseilles and get to Africa, the Legion will not send you back. If you can assume another identity and fool them here, you won't be pulled out later on."

Fingerprints were recorded and checked, as well as tattoos. In spite of this warning of the dangers of tattoos, some of the recruits were spending time carving them upon one another. They would sit in the shade of a parapet overlooking the bay and inscribe "Légion étrangère" or "Marseilles 1956" or just, "Le Legion." The operation was crude, using pocket knives or pens, plus a ball point pen or indelible pencil for coloring. I refused any free tattoo. I had made a big mistake, and a tattoo would be too much of an identification if I ever had to decamp in a hurry.

As I talked to the other recruits I realized that many were beginning to think as I did, that we had made a wrong move. I still hoped things would be better in Africa, and more like the soldiering I had dreamed of. I wanted to keep up a good front before the older men, especially since many liked to sneer at "soft Americans."

One of my chief gripes was the poor food, and on top of that, the battle to obtain the food, poor as it was. My training as a human being was going by the board. I was beginning to fight and threaten mayhem with the rest and best of the mob. One day Hans trod on my tender toes just as I was about to get a potato. I couldn't take time to retaliate then because I would miss out on grub. Later I pulled out my pocket knife and warned Hans, "Try that caper again and you'll be minus an ear." Hans just laughed, as if it were an idle threat. However, he stayed away from me for several days. Another time I almost came to blows over a crust of bread when I looked up and saw that my rival was Francesco. We grinned sheepishly, and later apologized. Was I becoming more of a man, or more of an animal?

Finally, we left. Carlos and I fell into ranks, were checked off the sergeant-chef's roster, and pushed into a canvas topped truck. Later, the trucks ground to a halt alongside a berth in Marseilles Harbor. Nearby was a ship that appeared to be a cross between a tramp steamer and a scow. I wondered if the tub would last the three days anticipated for our voyage to Africa.

We were herded like cattle into the hold of the cargo-passenger ship. Carlos and I were lucky. We managed to end up with canvas-backed sun deck chairs. The rest of the recruits were forced to sack out on deck on pieces of canvas. There seemed to be hundreds of Legionnaires crammed aboard. We were barely out of the harbor when dozens began to get seasick. They regurgitated where they lay, and it didn't take long for the jammed hold to become unbearable with the stench, heat, and mess.

I managed to get topside as much as possible during the three-day journey. We were allowed to walk on the forecastle, but never permitted to climb on the main deck where the passengers assembled. I longed to talk to a civilian. One lovely young lady must have noticed the pathetic expression on my face as I gazed up at her. *"Nous ferons une très mauvaise traversée,"* she said.

I figured she was trying to tell me that we were in for a rough trip, and tried to muster up my best, but not so fluent French. I was hoping to have her stay topside just so that I could look up at her. I tried to tell her that she should stay on deck because her stuffy cabin would make her ill.

"Je vous conseille de rester sur le pont. l'air de la cabine fermée pourrait vous rendre malade," I said.

My message got across because she started to chuckle. She was about to answer when a sous-officier jabbed me in the ribs with a nightstick and ordered me below decks. And that was the last I saw of the lovely young miss. However, the thought of her standing topside with her skirt blowing in the breeze helped make my voyage more bearable.

The food and sanitary conditions were just as bad as in the fort, with not enough of either to do the job intended. Adding to the discomfort aboard ship was the fact that while en route from one place to another, we were required to doff our coveralls, and don our wool uniforms, complete with green tie. The French were always conscious of how their soldiers looked in public.

All of these conditions caused our raw-edged nerves to become more sensitive. Fighting over the most picayune incident became more frequent. Ironically, the Legionnaires never seemed to argue or fight with another class of passengers jammed in the hold with us. These were several dozen Arabs, also going to Oran. I got along with them very well. It was hard to believe that within a short time I probably would be taking up arms against them. I had never seen an Arab before. Even with their tunics, robes, and baggy pants, there was something about them that seemed to demand respect.

My heart beat extra fast when I heard a call relayed from topside to the hold. "Land ahoy!" Carlos and I joined the crowd of Legionnaires on deck. No one said a word. We just stared at the shoreline with its silhouettes of towering ships' masts and buildings of assorted sizes and shapes in the background. If we peered through squinted eyes we could make out ant-like figures scurrying around the waterfront. It seemed like hours for the blue-green water gap of the Mediterranean to shrink. Eventually the sergeant-chef sounded l'appel and I found myself in formation with all my gear strapped to my back. Waiting seamen grabbed the starboard lines, quickly securing them to huge davits, and the ship slid into a smooth berthing. We were marched off the gangplank, and as I disembarked I glanced about hopefully for a last glimpse of the pretty passenger who had caught my eye the previous day. But she was nowhere to be seen. We were marched to a nearby fort. At our first meal here, and for the second time, I broke a tooth on the beans.

A few hours later we were on the move again. This time via truck to a railroad station, where we boarded an ancient coach that made the Toonerville Trolley look like the Empire State Express. Our destination was the famed headquarters of la Légion étrangère, Sidi Bel Abbes, some eighty miles southwest of Oran.

We were packed fifty to a coach for a train ride that extended overnight. Those fortunate enough to get aboard first slept three to a hard wooden seat. The rest slept on the floor. I was lucky enough to find an empty luggage rack. I managed to doze off with my pack as a pillow, and was awakened with a start when the train screeched to a halt. The sun was streaming through the windows. We had arrived. We were trucked to the Legion headquarters and unloaded inside the towering walls of a fort. I was not to get outside these walls until shipped to my next base.

CHAPTER 7

In Sidi Bel Abbes we were assigned to a CP, or *Companie de Passage,* a holding company for those in transit. Then it was back to the coveralls and the menial chores of cleaning quarters, latrines and kitchens. We also began learning French commands. The drill orders were shouted at us in French by the sous

"La droite!" yelled the corporal-chef. I didn't snap to attention at the instant the order was barked. I felt a burning sensation shoot through my head, and bright flashes danced before my eyes. When my vision came back into focus I found myself on the barracks floor looking up into the face of a snarling corporal. He was

holding his rifle by the barrel, with the stock a short distance from my head.

"What the hell was that for?" I started to protest, when a second smash across the side of my head forced my face down into the ancient planked floor. Carlos helped me to my feet and whispered in my ear, "Don't be a fool, mon ami. Say no more and follow instructions."

"The rest of you take note," warned the corporal. "You will respond to the commands without hesitation." We went to chow and my head still throbbed.

"How do you feel now, Ronnie?" Carlos asked.

"La douleur n'était pas aiguë, mais lancinante" I proudly answered in my best French. The pain was not acute, but throbbing. I was learning my French the hard way.

Conditions at Bel Abbes were better in some ways than at Marseilles. For one thing, we got more bread and pinard. The fort was much cleaner, too. We didn't have the unwanted insect problem that we had in Fort Nicholas. The bed chamber was typically Legion, with the same familiar fourteen-foot ceiling and musty brown walls, the single naked bulb in the middle of the chamber, and the few high windows at the end of the massive room. Every night we had *"Nettoyage de Chamber,"* or cleaning of the barracks. We swept, and then mopped the floor. Inspection was called while it was still wet. We stood at attention until the inspection was over.

The non-com in charge of our group was a German named Heinrich, who had served in the Legion for five years. He was rough, and in many instances, sadistic. He definitely was a throwback to his days as one of Hitler's SS Storm Troopers. The sergeant, who was the only one of us allowed to wear the kepi, or Legion cap, was typical of many a veteran Legionnaire. He was a homosexual, though Heinrich certainly was a far cry from the stateside type of homo. He was six-foot-three, and packed over two hundred and twenty-five pounds on his muscular frame. His hair was completely white, and he could have easily passed for a rough and tumble wrestling villain. Heinrich made me feel quite uneasy when he put his arm around me while ordering me to clean up the chamber. It wasn't unusual for him to belt me across the face with closed knuckles to expedite an order, while at the same time whispering out of the side of his mouth, *"Laissez--il rester tout seul avec moi, s'il est possible."* I had no intention of ever being found alone with him. He was as tough as nails, and took pleasure in brutality. Everyone was afraid of him, and for good reason.

I dare say, from what I witnessed in the Legion, more than half of the Legionnaires went in for homosexual practices. The majority of the Legionnaires had little contact with women for as long as two years at a stretch. They were either fighting in the desert, spending their time on work details, or restricted to the fort. Although everyone knew of the goings on, it was never discussed. Several Legionnaires that I knew were caught in embarrassing positions by the French officers, and sent to remote desert outposts as punishment. One Belgian was involved, a leader in a tank group, who had been decorated for valor in battle. Still another was a giant of a German, who would just as soon cut your throat as look at you. He did just that more than a dozen times while in combat with the Arab rebels. The primary rule was, "Don't get caught in the act."

The weeks at Sidi Bel Abbes went slowly. When there were no work details available we were kept busy on the Legion's version of the old rock pile. Instead of breaking big rocks into little ones, were led to a huge pile of metal. I swung a large sledge and tackled the cast iron mountain. The small pieces we accumulated were used for smelting. It was a tedious task. It was impossible to get into a comfortable position while reducing a large piece of metal. I would shift from one knee to the other, and finally end up in a sitting position.

Money was somewhat of a problem, although I wasn't going any place. Pay during the instruction period came to about three dollars a month. Some of the men were getting an enlistment bonus. This was the inducement that had caused some to join. The bonus ran to around thirty to forty thousand francs, one hundred American dollars. The money was paid after six months in the Legion. Perhaps it was believed that if a man got it sooner he might desert. Some of the men did not qualify for this bonus, although I couldn't see why. Others were cheated out of it. I knew one sous-officier who was embezzling bonus money from the recruits. The sous-officiers, or noncoms, had a great deal of power. We privates would call them, secretly, "mon con," or "my fool." The noncom's favorite term for us was "Koko" or monkey.

Our treatment in Africa wasn't any different than it had been in France. It was the usual degrading details and abuse. I continued thinking of a way to escape. I heard of three Germans who had escaped while out on the firing range. No one ever heard from them again. Later the noncoms said the men had been killed. We didn't know if this were true, or if they made this up to discourage the rest of us from taking off.

On another occasion I was given the job of delivering coal to the house of a sous-officier. As was the custom, an old Legionnaire was sent along with every bleu. While we were getting the coal an Arab sidled up to the ancien, slipped him a note and then disappeared. The veteran, a German, said the note stated that life was dreadful in the Legion, and if anyone would join the Arabs, he would be helped to get home. The German destroyed the note. He would have none of it. He was an old veteran of Hitler's World War 11 army.

When the five weeks were up, we packed our gear once more and got ready for our next move. Our destination was Mascara, for four months of infantry training. Mascara is a town and Legion post in Algeria, about one hundred miles east of Sidi Bel Abbes. The trip was made by truck caravan, and in the usual wool uniforms. Our first view of Mascara was truly dismal. The October rain had a chill to it, and the only sign of vegetation was the scrubby remains of what once was a tree.

Hans put his arm around me and said, "The Legion is good, eh, Ronnie? *Vous allez la Légion.*" He was rubbing it in that the Legion was rough and I didn't fit the part. I could hardly believe that the outlook could seem so forlorn, and especially to me, at nineteen, and in the Legion less than two months. I knew that I couldn't spend the next five years subjected to brutal discipline, an animal-like existence, rotten and meager food, filth, pestilence, and the possibility of a lonely death -- death in a worthless cause far from the freedom, comfort, and love of my home and family, who didn't even know I was a mercenary in the French Foreign Legion. I knew then that escape and desertion lie dormant in the minds of most Legionnaires. The idea was entering my every thought. I had a perpetual urge for freedom. I realized that the chance of escaping was slim. If I weren't killed by the animals in the desert, the Arab rebels would see to it that the job was completed. They might do this for spite or revenge, or for the bounty my carcass would get them from the Legion. If I were captured and returned alive, my chances of surviving the dreaded penal institutions were also slight. These thoughts tumbled through my mind as the truck caravan approached the fort. My mind was definitely made up. I was going to make a break for it soon.

Carlos and Dominic flanked me in the cramped truck. Dominic apparently detected my despondency and tried to perk me up.

"Eh Ron, compadre, cheer up. Pretty soon you may see *bella signora*. We get him nice girls. Eh Carlos?"

Carlos flashed his white teeth and quipped. "In time, mon ami, in time. We will invade the bordellos like the three Musketeers." Those two wonderful guys lifted my spirits, and my heart wasn't quite so heavy when we piled out of the truck inside the prison-like walls.

We were led to our chamber, which was like those in the other forts. My billet was on the fourth floor. Carlos and Francesco were in my group. I unpacked my gear and stood in front of my bunk for muster. Second-hand uniforms were issued to us. These new woolens would allow for *"commine de combat."* Also issued was the long awaited kepi, the Legion type combat cap.

"Sergeant," I asked, "Where is the white neck cloth for my kepi?"

"Ho, Ho, child," he answered mockingly. "The *couvre nuque* went out of existence about the time of the bustle." I also learned to my disappointment that the capote, or Legion tunic of bright blue, and the red baggy pants also were a dress of the legendary past.

For the first time we got a weapon, a trente-six or MOS 36 rifle, meaning a 1936 model. It was 7.5 caliber, weighed about eight pounds, and had a five shot clip and needle bayonet.

We went to evening mess and had the usual potatoes, gravy, bread and wine. Then the sous-officier in charge of our group gave us a break and told us that there would be no details that day. Reveille the next day would be at 5:30, followed by a day jammed with instruction, training and details.

This was the first time I felt I really had to write a letter home. Every day it became more necessary for me to write, but I dreaded to begin. How could I ever tell my folks that I was in the French Foreign Legion, and would be for the next five years- if I survived. They still thought I was touring Europe. I must have started a half dozen letters. They seemed so morbid and despondent that I tore them into bits and tried again. One could get so sentimental longing for what had been taken for granted through the years. My parents had to know something about my condition, but I had to be careful not to grieve them more than necessary.

Mascara, Algeria October 28, 1956

Dear Mom and Dad,

I am deeply sorry that it has been so long since I have last written you. I have joined the French Foreign Legion. Because of this I could not write until now. It has been an equally long time since I have slept in peace, and I always knew it was because I knew you were longing and wondering. I enlisted September 10, 1965, just five months since my departure from home. I did not want to write until my enlistment was final. Men were turned away constantly in the beginning, and thus I did not write. At present I think I am well in. I enlisted in Paris. From there I was sent to Marseilles, and then on to Sidi Bel Abbes in Africa. Just today I arrived here in Mascara where I will commence with the primary training. It's taken much time to reach this point, almost two months. I came to Europe, in fact I left for Florida, with this intention of entering the Legion. The five months of wandering was only a postponement of the act. It was just one more chance for overcoming this defeating temperament I have, and as so many times in the past, I lost. Thus I am here. The life in the Legion is not easy. But I deserve the whole future that the Legion will inevitably offer, because I have had too many gracious chances before, all given to me through your love and God's tolerance. I should thus always consider this the reward for my ungratefulness. I think of you more than ever before in my life. You are always with me. I do not want to sound sad, yet I can only write of my heart at this time. Please believe me, my greatest regret is for you, Mother and Dad, my absolute deepest regret. Give sister Sue and Grandma and Pa my love. The Legion reads our mail, but it does not matter. I am sorry. I will sleep better now, I know. Please write to me Mom and Dad. The Legion sends the mail, but I don't know if by air or ship.

I love you always,

Your son, Ronnie
Legionnaire R.E. Reynolds

I knew that I would finally be able to sleep in peace this night. The letter home was the purgative I so badly needed. I longed more than ever now to hear from my loved ones so very far away. They were in my heart and thoughts as I dropped off to sleep.

Legionnaire Ronald Reynolds earns the right to wear his white Kepi hat after six months of training with an armored unit of the Legion

CHAPTER 8

The shrill whistle before sunrise brought me to the deck in one bound. A corporal-chef barked orders for us to make our sacks and prepare for *casse-croute,* or breakfast. I dressed in my coveralls, rolled up my bedding, freshened up as best I could, and marched into the dining hall. Breakfast was no different again, with a hunk of bread, a morsel of cheese, a couple of sardines, and black coffee.

Next we assembled for our first assignment. In our *caserne,* or fort, which was the smaller of the two strongholds in Mascara, there were two companies of Legionnaires. Each company had four sections of about twenty-five men. In turn, the individual section was composed of four *equipes,* or squads. I was assigned to the fourth section of the second company, which was commanded by Captain Le Blanc.

On this and succeeding days we were marched to the outskirts of town for instruction. While marching to and from the training area we sang Legion songs. One popular tune was *"Le Boudin,"* or *"The Blood Sausage."* Others were, *"We Are All Volunteers," "White Kepi," "Under The Brilliant Sun Of Africa," "In Algeria,"* and *"Veronica."* The Legion marches slowly when it is not in combat operations. The marching, combined with the singing, began to develop a bit of *esprit de corps.* We began to feel we were members of an outstanding unit. Later, this feeling began to ebb.

We lined up in the courtyard and marched some two miles to a farm area designated specifically for our training. Part of the training site consisted of small buildings for instructions. There also was a firing range, which took up some of our time. Our instructors concentrated on teaching the French language. We rotated from one classroom to another. In addition to the French, our sous-officier instructors conducted classes in the manual of arms, the nomenclature of the equipment, rules for guard duty, classes in grenade throwing, and the history of the Legion. The story is shrouded in some secrecy. An outsider can only accept hearsay as his knowledge of the Legion. There are no records available to an outsider. Its history has been written in blood, by mercenaries of all nationalities, creeds, and from all walks of life.

The French Foreign Legion had its inception on March 10, 1831 by a royal decree of Louis Philippe, King of France. During the next 130 years of its existence, the Legion had a record of almost continuous fighting. It became one of the greatest forces in history. Daring and courage were commonplace. It is believed to have the highest mortality rate of any military unit. Estimates on deaths in the first five-year enlistment range up to ninety percent, and some say a conservative guess would be over half. Legion strength and casualties are not publicized. In 1956, there were probably about forty thousand men in the Legion. Louis Philippe incorporated existing bands of mercenaries into one army under the name of *la Légion étrangère*. It was patterned after the Legion D'Honneur lobe, which fought during the Napoleonic wars.

The Legion was formed originally to fight for France and Algeria. A major factor leading to its formation occurred in the summer of 1827. Two seemingly insignificant and amusing incidents played a key role. It seems that the ruler of Algeria, Dey Hussein, was being pestered by flies. Adding to his discomfort was the fact that the French Consul was chastising him for attacking French merchant ships. The short tempered Dey grabbed his royal fly swatter and smashed it across the face of the Consul. This international incident gave France the excuse it sought to invade Algeria. French war ships landed in 1830, and Algeria surrendered. In that year Louis Philippe took over the throne of France from Charles X during a revolution. Although French troops still held the coast of Algeria, conditions were a bit unsteady. Since there weren't many French volunteers, Louis Philippe recruited foreigners, and gave them security while they fought the Moors in Africa under the French flag. Thus was born the army of phantoms--in their legendary baggy red trousers, blue tunic and kepi with its flowing white linen neckpiece--charging against odds under the banner of the tri-color. The Legion was born in Algeria and did its last major fighting there. In its first battle in Algeria in the early 1830's, the brave mercenaries were to experience the first of many defeats by an enemy that outnumbered them by many to one. But from their first defeat at Constantine by Arab leader Abd-EI Kader, and through the years, they continued to chill the blood of their enemies by countless acts of bravery as they fought to the death.

Over an hour had passed during my first instruction on the history of the Legion by a French captain. Suddenly I longed to know more about the mysterious army I had voluntarily joined. I still felt hate for the Legion, and craved freedom more than ever, but there was some strange, proud feeling within when I heard about my predecessors in the Legion of the Damned. We took a break for lunch and I filled my plate with the meatless stew slop and sat next to Carlos on an ammunition case.

"What do you think, Carlos? Are we being brainwashed?"

"To some extent, Ronnie," he replied. "The purpose is to instill in you the so-called esprit de corps you American Marines are famous for."

I ate the rest of my chow in silence, then joined the rest of the recruits for the second session on the history of the Legion.

Although the Legion suffered heavy losses in its first major battle, Louis Philippe managed to recruit enough men to fill the void in the ranks. It took three years to rebuild the Legion, only to have it sent to Spain and experience another butchering. By this time, things were operating better, and there were fewer casualties.

Louis Philippe loaned the entire French Foreign Legion to the Spanish Queen Regent, Maria Christina, in 1835, in an effort to prevent Don Carlos from seizing the throne vested by the death of his brother, King Ferdinand VII. The Civil War lasted a year with no conclusive victory for either side. Philippe finally recalled his Legion. Of the three thousand troops sent in, only 222 survived. Those that weren't killed in battle died of disease and malnutrition. It seemed that neither Philippe nor Queen Regent Maria wanted to pay the fighting men, much less clothe and feed them. The half-dead survivors returned to France and were again reformed for the conquest of Algeria.

I was so absorbed in the class that I was surprised when the officers told us that the session was over until the next day. We finished out the afternoon in other skill work sessions. It was time for the march back to the fort, and the sergeant-chef ordered us to fall in. We really sounded like proud Legionnaires when we struck up the song of the first foreign regiment, "We Are Volunteers."

"Nous Sommes Tous Des Volontaires" -- We are all volunteers. *"Nous marchons gaiement en cadence"*-- We march happily in cadence. *"Malgré le vent et malgré la pluie"*-- Despite the wind and despite the rain. *"Les meilleurs soldats de la France"* -- The best soldiers of France. *"Etes-avant, maintenant, regardez-nous"* -- Are before you, now, look at us. *"Nous Sommes Tous Des Volontaires"* -- We are all volunteers. *"Les hommes du premier régiment de la Légion"* -- The men of the first regiment of the Legion. *"Notre devise est légendaire"* -- Our motto is legendary. *"Honor, la fidélité, la fidélité"* -- Honor, fidelity, fidelity. *"Mars sur, Légionnaires"*-- March on, Légionnaires. *"Dans la boue, dans le sable brillant"* -- In the mud, in the brilliant sand. *"Mars avec l'âme de lumière"* -- March with light soul. *"Et cœur vaillant"*-- And valiant heart. *"Mars sur, Légionnaires"*-- March on, Legionnaires.

We were getting some spirit, but I still wanted out. We reached the fort, cleaned up and had "soupe" at six pm. We were on our own then, but most of us were so exhausted that we hit the sack early. We were not allowed out on pass during the training period.

The next day we began with weapons. It seemed good to fire a gun again. I was judged the best shot in my section on the rifle range, and I could thank my hunting experience with Dad for that.

"Voici votre prix, Reynolds," commented the sergeant-chef, "Here is your prize." Next to a discharge, I couldn't think of a better reward, a bottle of cold beer. Next came the class on grenades. This was followed by more range work, this time using machine guns. Here I did not fare as well.

Then it was back to the classroom for lessons in French Legion history. We went back to the year 1837 when France was still endeavoring to take over Algeria. So it was back to the walled city of Constantine, which was held by Moslem leader Abd-El Kader. The brave Arabs, who believed in eternal salvation surrounded by dancing girls if they died in battle, fought fanatically. The Legion finally took the city after hand-to-hand, and house-to-house combat, which pitted the Legion's bayonets against the Arab swords. El Kader fled into the mountains and directed sporadic attacks against the French for the next fifteen years. The Arabs tortured and killed their prisoners. The Arab women were more barbaric and relished, on occasion, the mutilation of their captives, especially when they were still alive. Since that time, the unwritten code of the Legion has been to never leave their dead unburied. Scores of instances are recorded, describing how the grim faced Legionnaires raced into bullets and swords to bring back the fallen bodies of their comrades. During some encounters the enemy was so awestruck by the heroic deeds, that they held their fire and cheered the Legionnaires as they carried off their dead.

When not fighting, the Legionnaires were sent to grueling construction work in the desert, building roads, forts, schools and railroads. The Legionnaires also dug wells, laid out parks, planted trees and drained swamps. Things were rather quiet for the Legion, with the exception of minor skirmishes, until the Crimean War. Russian Czar Nicholas I had his eye on the Turkish Empire, and Britain objected because a victory would place the Russians too close to Egypt and India. Napoleon III of France had delusions of grandeur and volunteered his fighting Foreign Legion to back up Britain.

In 1854 the Legion's first regiment landed at Gallipoli. The invasion was costly to the aggressors, but the heavy death toll didn't come from enemy gunfire. Cholera struck, and the disease cut a deep swath into the Legion line. There weren't many survivors aboard ship for the crossing of the Black Sea to invade the Russian city of Sevastopol. The fighting forces landed and made a slow advance during heavy fighting. Legionnaires were felled by bullets, disease, and the bitter elements. Malnutrition took a heavy toll. Despite these obstacles, victory was won at the battles of Alma and Inkerman. Nicholas died, peace was restored, and it was back to Africa again for the Legion, where the Arabs were restless once more. However, Napoleon III managed to scrape up another war for the Legion.

The year was 1858, and most of Italy was divided, with Austria controlling the north. Two provinces on the French border appealed to the French ruler. So it was across the Mediterranean and bitter hand to-hand fighting with the tough Austrians. Victory again was won, after much bloodshed. Power hungry Louis Napoleon hoped for a new empire in the New World. With America involved in a Civil War, he figured that the Monroe Doctrine wouldn't stand up. He decided to conquer Mexico, but figured wrong in assuming that the Mexicans would welcome a monarchy. His plan was to hand the Mexican throne to Archduke Maximilian of Austria, the brother of the man he defeated in Italy, Franz Josef. From the invasion of Mexico comes the most sacred battle in Legion history. It was fought on April 30, 1863 in Camarón, Mexico. This famous stand was similar to our battle at the Alamo. In both cases, the slaughter to the last brave soldier came at the hands of the Mexicans.

The famed Captain Danjou, with a wooden hand replacing the one he left in battle with the Russians, was in charge of a band of sixty Legionnaires. The convoy of pack horses the Legion escorted through Camarón carried three million francs, which were to be paid to the French troops fighting deep in the interior of Mexico near Vera Cruz. The sixty Legionnaires were ambushed by two hundred Mexican cavalrymen. The French mercenaries formed a circle with their horses and cargo as protection, and fought valiantly. They were holding their own against three-to-one odds, when a second Mexican cavalry group rode into the outskirts of Camarón and joined in the attack. The surviving Legionnaires made a break for it and took refuge in a barn. Then the sound of a distant bugle was heard, the trapped Legionnaires rejoiced. But their joy was short lived, when it dawned on them that the bugle calls were strange. Their fears were confirmed when hundreds more Mexicans stormed into view. Mexican General Milan called for Captain Danjou to surrender. The odds were two thousand to a handful. The small band of Legionnaires took an oath to fight to the end. They repelled charge after charge. The captain was mortally wounded and his lieutenant took command. The end was much nearer when the Mexicans set fire to the barn. The brave Legion patrol, down to six men, fixed bayonets and charged out of the barn into the gunfire of two thousand Mexicans. Two were killed and four were wounded. One of the wounded was left for dead, and the three others were taken captive. The half-dead survivor was found by a relief force, along with fifty-six dead Legionnaires and three hundred dead Mexicans. The anniversary of the battle of Camarón is a hallowed day in the Legion, and is observed every April 30th. In the Hall of Honor at Sidi Bel Abbes-- amid many citations, medals, and flags won by heroes who fought and died--in the place of honor and distinction is the wooden hand of Captain Danjou. After this battle, in 1885, the Legion was sent to Indochina and was to serve there until the 1950's. Our lecture was over for the day, and my belief in the Legion's fighting ability was growing. I only hoped I could survive my *"bapteme du feu,"* baptism of fire.

After soupe we went back to the rifle range for another session. Ammunition was always scarce, and this factor helped make us sharpshooters. We were to make every shot count and waste no rounds. A veteran sergeant-chef, who had fought in the Indochina theater two years previous, was stressing the correct form and procedure. We had to learn to follow instructions at the drop of a hand. I was ordered to hit the deck and freeze, but was a bit slow in responding.

The sergeant-chef barked, *"Couchez-vous! Ne bougez pas!"* I threw myself on the ground, my rifle in front of me, and waited for the next order. My big mistake was in raising my head a few inches to get a better view of the terrain. It was at that instant that a hobnailed boot crashed into the side of my helmet.

"*Cochon!*" screamed the sous-officier. "*Ne bougez pas!*" I learned faster from then on. We continued to rotate for the various phases of instruction.

It felt good to crawl into my sack that night. I just managed to finish my second letter home before lights out.

Mascara, Algerie
End of November 1956

Dear Mom and Dad,

Receiving your last letters of the 14th and 23rd was the finest thing that's happened to me in a very long time. Life here is like living in a different world. Time passes so slow here that I have lost all track of a certain day's individuality, such as Dad's and Sue's birthdays, Thanksgiving Day and all. They keep you busy all the time, but it is like the work of a stoker who must keep shoveling and shoveling.

And, my very beloved parents, you can't realize how much I long for you. Many leave here, but are most always brought back. Thank you for wanting to send me something Mom, but I need nothing materially, and the next thing

I receive from you, I want to take from your own hands.

If I had done what you told me and been an obedient son, I would have been a happy guy. Love is the thing, the gift, that makes the life worthwhile, and the person an individual. So without this, life seems plenty cheap, and then once in the Legion, it's minimized to the lowest of low value. But for me, this experience is good and necessary. It is bitter medicine, but the cure in the end will have been worth the terrible taste. So it is not that I am sorry that I must do what I am now doing, my regret is that I require such stern measures to give me a righteous sense of values and balanced outlook on life. But I am very fortunate to have the consolations of good health, and most important of all, the hope of being with you again, Mom and Dad, knowing that you will be waiting for me.

Your son,
Ronnie

Type of vehicle Ron operated during cavalry
training in Sidi Bel AbbesIt's an American made
A.M. used to lead and guard convoys.

CHAPTER 9

It was 10 PM and the barracks fell silent as the single bare light was put out. I must have fallen asleep seeing as my head touched the ticking. What seemed like seconds later, but actually was an hour, several shrill blasts from a whistle and the light going on brought us all suddenly awake. Stunned, and groggy with sleep, we were ordered to general quarters. Several officers and noncoms stormed into the room and we were ordered to dress for combat.

"*Vite! Vite! Aux armes!*" was the command. "*Vite!* "As I jumped into my uniform and checked my rifle, I turned to Carlos.

"What gives Carlos? Where are we going? Who are we going to fight?"

"This is your 'bapteme du feu.' But never fear, it is probably a mission to frighten some Arab farmer who is sympathetic to the rebels and supplies them with his crops."

I was both thrilled and a bit frightened at the thought of my first combat with the rebel Arabs, known as the Fellagha. They were the notorious members of the N.L.F., the National Liberation Front.

We assembled in the courtyard, and I didn't know if the shiver that went through my bones was from the near-frigid damp weather or from apprehension. We were handed ammunition and ordered forward.

"En avant par deux!" yelled the lieutenant, and we were off to our first skirmish.

One of the sous-officiers walked up and down the ranks as we marched to our destination, filling us in with the object of our mission. We were en route to a farmhouse four miles away, in which it was believed several members of the NLF were hiding out. It was about two in the morning when our platoon surrounded the ramshackle building. The lieutenant kicked in the front door as the sergeant-chef crashed in the rear. At a given signal half of the platoon converged on the shed-like dwelling while the rest of us spaced off and ringed the plank structure.

The screams of a half a dozen women and four elderly men made my hair stand on end. The gruff Legionnaires manhandled the terrified Arab women, who clutched naked children in their arms. The lieutenant demanded to know the whereabouts of the younger men. Somehow they had gotten wind of the coming attack and had fled to the hills.

It was then that I got my first bitter taste of Legion retaliation. The women, aged and crippled, men, and children were routed from the house. Then three Legionnaires set the house afire, torched the crops, and killed six chickens, which went into the knapsacks of officers and noncoms. Also confiscated were vegetables and fruits raised by the farm women in the absence of their men, who had joined rebel bands in the hills.

Then came the order to round up the prisoners. Some stood by the flaming debris screaming, while others tried to run off. I hustled several into the group of prisoners waiting to be marched back to the fort. A big Spaniard by the name of Raphael let out a whoop. He was chasing a rather pretty teen-aged Arab girl, who was doing a fair job of eluding her panting pursuer, much to the delight of the howling Legionnaires. Carlos and I were the only ones who didn't enjoy the sight of the pitiful young girl trying desperately to avoid the outstretched arms of the wild-eyed Raphael.

Then the poor creature stumbled over a rock and Raphael panted wildly as he fell on top of her. I expected

Raphael to pick up the girl and push her into line with the other prisoners, but he had other plans. He tore off her clothing in two sweeps of his big hands. I couldn't believe my eyes. Before I realized it, I was running toward Raphael and his victim screaming, "Raphael, stop! You rotten pig! Cochon! Leave her alone!" He paid no attention to me or the girl's pathetic screams and moans. He was too occupied in ravishing her. He was not even aware of the cheering Legionnaires who ringed the scene of conquest and shouted obscene suggestions. I had dropped my rifle and sprinted to within ten yards of the thrashing bodies, when an iron grip on my shoulder stopped me dead in my tracks with a jolt. It was Carlos.

"No, no mon ami. It is best not to interfere. There are some things revolting to our nature that we can do nothing about. If you stop that swine, his knife would be sure to find you out some night when you were asleep."

"My God, Carlos, civilized men do not do these things. It is savage. Look, even the so-called honorable French officers turn their backs on this atrocity."

I took one last look back as Carlos led me to the prisoners and their guards, and caught sight of Raphael slowly rising, breathing in gasps and wiping the grimy sweat from his brow with the sleeve of his tunic. The girl on the ground uttered a sobbing sound. Then her bruised body twitched spastically before suddenly becoming very still. She was dead. She was left there, to be buried by the menfolk, who would return from the hills after we departed. I was sick. The dead girl was about the same age as my sister.

I didn't sing with the group on the return trip. My heart wasn't in it. We were told we could sleep later in the morning. As tired as I was I couldn't drop off into slumber. All I could see when I closed my eyes was the frightened Arab girl.

The next day I still refrained from song as we marched. The slow cadence reminded me of a funeral dirge. The morning was spent on the obstacle course. Two of the recruits tried to tackle the high wall, and fell back to the ground with broken arms. I was lucky. I found that by crashing against the concrete barrier as high as possible, I was able to use the momentum to actually crawl up the smooth surface a couple of feet until I could grab the top and swing myself over. I thank my stars I was in good physical shape. I managed to get through the rest of the course of hurdles, pits, barbed fences, and other obstacles, fairly well. Some of the older recruits collapsed or suffered seizures.

After lunch we were back in the classroom for more Legion history. The next phase was World War 1. One of the first Legion heroes was an American from Brooklyn named Russell Kelly. He sailed to France on a cattle boat and enlisted. His action in the face of the enemy is legendary. They still talk about his hand-to-hand combat with jabbing bayonet, leaping from one hole to another as bullets tore past him and bombs burst at his feet. Before being killed in action, Kelly lasted long enough to receive the highest French awards for valor.

An American group that became known all over the world was the famed flying squadron, or Escadrille that thrilled and shocked both enemy and fellow Legionnaires by its devil-may-care attitude and skill and bravery in battle. The 38 American pilots secured 57 confirmed victories. When the U.S. entered the war, the Lafayette Escadrille formed the 103 Pursuit Squadron of the U.S. Air Corps.

In World War II, Germans in the Legion were given a choice of going home, or serving in Africa. Many volunteered to fight the Nazi symbol they hated and had fled from. In 1940, a Legion group gained fame for its firm stand at Dunkirk. The small, gallant band held off many Germans while the British forces were evacuating. The bridge at Dunkirk was blown up at the last minute to keep the enemy from crossing into the French city before the evacuation was completed. With the fall of France, the surviving Legionnaires headed back to Sidi Bel Abbes. In 1942 the Legion joined in the fight against Rommel. By this time the Legion had become mechanized.

In December 1956 I had completed three months in the Legion and was convinced that I could never serve out my five-year enlistment. The groundwork already was laid for my bid for freedom. On one of my passes into town I had managed to bribe a colonist into giving me his civilian clothing, which included his beret and sunglasses. I stashed them in an olive grove at the far end of town. On my next furlough I went into Mascara and spent most of my time in bistros, stoking up courage to make the trip.

It was about ten at night when I stepped out into the nearly bare streets. I was still in uniform, heading away from the fort toward the olive grove, when my blood went cold. A Legion sous-officier was heading in my direction. There was no time for panic now. I figured that the best I could do was to act nonchalant and pass him by. As I started by him I smiled and nodded, and much to my surprise, he did likewise. Apparently the noncom thought I was a French soldier going to a small Legion depot beyond the olive grove. What saved me was the fact that I had taken off the white cover from my kepi, showing only the blue base. A French officer's cap has a blue base with a little red trim. I was over the first hurdle, but the race was far from won.

I reached the olive grove and buried my Legion outfit. I had a pinard of wine to ward off the chill of the near-freezing temperature. My scanty civilian clothing was not a good match for the elements, and I shivered the entire night on the frosty ground. It was a long night, made even more. lengthy by my anxiety and expectation, and I only caught snatches of sleep. When dawn finally arrived, I walked out of the orchard in my civilian baggy trousers, shirt, beret, sunglasses and sandals. I hoped I looked like a French civilian. I headed straight for the heart of town.

Approaching the bus depot, I spotted walking toward me Corporal-Chef Swartz, a fifteen-year noncom from my section. There was no turning back now. I kept my eyes dead ahead and walked right past Swartz. He didn't even glance at me. My disguise had passed the first test. I walked into the station and blurted forth what I had memorized over and over. *"Un ticket. S'il vous plaît"*

I boarded the old bus, which was crowded with many Arabs and a few Frenchmen. My next worry was being stopped at one of the control posts along the road. It was customary for the police to make spot checks of all travelers for their credentials. Everyone in Algeria had an identification card. If he didn't, it meant he was fighting with the Arabs in the mountains. Because of the revolution, the French colonists, or colons, needed I.D. cards as well as the Arabs. Ordinarily, the gendarmes at regulation control points stopped vehicles and pedestrians to make a check. However, in the long trip, our bus wasn't stopped once.

When I arrived in Oran I got another rude jolt that left me in near panic. There was no U.S. consulate in Oran. The nearest one was three hundred miles east, in Algiers. I was desperate. I wandered about Oran trying to find a solution. My big mistake was in not checking around the docks for a neutral ship.

Instead, I headed for the train depot and purchased a ticket for Algiers. My only hope was to make contact with the American Consul there. I was sure the U.S. government could get me out of the Legion.

I had an eight-hour wait for the train, so I decided to look up the family of a Legion buddy. A taxi took me to a stucco type row house in the suburbs. Monsieur Paul and his wife took me in with open arms. They gave me warm clothing and fed me the best meal I had had in three months. They went all the way to make me comfortable until train time.

"God be with you, my son," said Paul as he saw me aboard. "Be very careful" cautioned his wife as she put a bottle of wine and a loaf of hot bread in my arms.

"Thank you, and may God bless you," I shouted as the screeching train started on its way.

I no sooner settled back in the stiff-backed seat when the coach door swung open and two gendarmes began a methodical check of each passenger. I was frozen with fear and just sat there helplessly when they approached me.

"Votre identification?" asked the burly policeman.

In my poor French I stuttered that I must have misplaced it. I was yanked to my feet, and his probing hands went through my pockets. I was petrified when he came up with my prize possessions, two letters from my parents. They were addressed to Legionnaire Ronald Reynolds, 114685. It was all over. One of the gendarmes stuck a pistol in my face and ordered me into a nearby compartment. Another gendarme in civilian clothing got into the act.

"*Saloud Cachon!*" he screamed, and beat me in the face and stomach until I blacked out. The gendarme, who definitely was anti-American, shook me conscious and kept calling me a traitor while he continued to pound on my face until it was nothing but pulp. He threatened to shoot me time and time again. If it weren't for the uniformed officer, he would have. The unmerciful beating continued for more than an hour.

"I will kill you, you traitor, you deserter!" he screamed.

"Go ahead, you bastard, go ahead!" I cried. Then I blacked out again.

I was awakened by the train coming to a halt at a little town. The gendarme dragged me to the prison office and turned me over to the local chief for escort back to the fort. The chief and his deputy treated me well, in sharp contrast to what I expected. They fixed me up in a nice warm cell and bedded me down for the night. The chief's wife brought in a good hot meal, which I managed to enjoy despite my battered face and throbbing stomach and ribs. It seemed like minutes later that the sun lit up the cell. The chief came for me and we boarded a bus back to Mascara.

"Here, Reynolds, let me take the handcuffs off. I've fixed a box lunch for you."

"Thanks chief, I guess all of you gendarmes aren't like the gorillas aboard the train." The chief merely smiled and let me enjoy my snack in silence, as the bus chugged its way over the dusty countryside, taking me back to what awaited me. I tried not to think about it.

CHAPTER 10

I entered the prison fort at Mascara, and was escorted to the Poste de Police. A Legion veteran on duty had me ushered before him. The first thing he did was to grab my civilian hat and slam me across the face with it.

"Swine of a traitor, you will pay dearly for your cowardly act!" The guard was joined by the sous-officier in charge, and the interrogation began. The sergeant was a huge Turk with a sweeping black mustache and wild piercing brown eyes.

"Where did you get the civilian clothes?" he demanded.

"I bought them from a stranger," I answered. A series of blows to the face and stomach sent me crashing to the floor.

"Again, I want to know, where did you get the clothes?" I could barely get the words past my swollen lips.

"I didn't know his name," I gasped. A thick boot caught me on the side of my head, and the room began to spin dizzily in flashing multicolored lights, as I vomited and my head dropped in my own mess.

It must have been hours later when I awoke in an unfamiliar place. It was dark, but I could make out my surroundings. I was in a small dungeon-like cell with overhead bars looking out into the black and gloomy sky. My bed was a wooden plank. I curled up into a ball for warmth, and fell into a stupor until morning.

The new dawn found a guard yanking me to my feet and dragging me to the non com's office. The Turk was a sergeant-chef who had served with the Germans in World War II. There was no doubt he remembered a few tricks of the trade for his sadistic role in the Legion.

The towering Turk eyed me contemptuously and snarled, "Well, Reynolds, it seems that you have to be taught a few manners. We have just the cure for you. See out this window? It is our exercise pit for the likes of you. I am sure that after eight or ten hours around, you will see things differently."

The cinder track was about sixteen yards in circumference, and ten yards wide in the design of the Legion emblem--a grenade with shooting flames. It was like a blown-up *fleur de lis*. Six prisoners were running around the track, each staggering under a fifty-pound log on his shoulder. A seventh inmate was carrying a seventy-five pound jagged boulder. At odd intervals there would be a brief break, designed to get the men to fight among themselves. The mad Turk got quite a kick out of the seven miserable souls scrambling for the six logs. The unfortunate seventh man would find only the flesh-biting rock left for his burden. The Turk smiled at me and barked, "Now, Reynolds, down to the pit with you. We have a freshly cut log just for you."

"I won't go," I mumbled. The upturned mustache twitched violently, and his burning eyes flashed dangerously. The Turk regained some composure at this unaccustomed affront. Then he sneered. In an instant his hammer-like fist slammed into my nose. Another savage blow caught me in the gut, and again I was back on the floor. The blurred room was spinning, but I did manage to catch ᵃ glimpse of a large boot plummeting toward my face. I managed to twist my head, and received only a glancing blow. But it was enough to send me into blackness.

I was slapped into consciousness and dragged to my feet.

"What is your answer now, Reynolds?" demanded the Turk.

"I'm on my way," I sputtered, and staggered out doors to the torture pit.

The prisoners stumbled around the pit with dead eyes staring into space. We were all stripped to the waist, and to make sure we really had a rough time navigating, our shoe laces were removed. This torturous trek was enjoyed by the Turk, who would stand alongside the track and scream at us to break into a trot. He drank all day, and the more wine he had the more vicious he became. As I passed him he would lash out at me with a whip. When I fell to the sharp cinders, he would strike me with the switch, and tear into my ribs with his boots. Then would come the occasional break, followed by a whistle blast, which set off the mad scramble for the logs. The loser wound up with the boulder. This was typical of Legion tactics-- have the men fight among themselves. During one of my staggering rounds under a blistering sun in ninety- degree heat, my tongue was so swollen from thirst that I was nearly choking to death.

"Mon Dieu," I cried, "I must have some water!" One of the guards stepped forward with a bucket and scooped out its contents with a ladle. It was salted water, which caused me to throw up a slimy green bile into the large spoon.

"Hoi" hollered the guard. "You would waste our precious water!" The next moment he forced me to drink up the mess that I had caused. This made me even sicker. A sadistic prank played by the guards was to have us lean forward against a wall with our weight resting on our outstretched hands. Then they would take delight in kicking our feet out from under us, dropping us face first into the cinders.

This went on for ten days. In the first five days, our only food was a daily portion of a small piece of bread and a cup of greasy soup. I lost weight and began to suffer from dysentery. After the five days, our meals were increased to half the rations we normally would be served at the fort. The starvation diet played havoc with my digestive system. We were allowed toilet privileges only once a day. On occasion I would sneak a nightly defecation. This had to be deposited in my mess tin, which would be hidden until morning, and then washed with our breakfast utensils. One evening a fellow prisoner wasn't discreet enough to secrete his discharge. A corporal-chef making his rounds found the evidence, and demanded to know who the culprit was. We were all silent.

"If none of you swine own up to this, you will all suffer!" screamed the corporal. No one volunteered any information, and we all were forced to eat a share of the disgusting mess.

There were about twenty prisoners in the prison at one time or another during my month-long stay. Two prisoners died at the hands of the Turk, and a third, a Spaniard, disappeared. The last time we saw Chico he was brought before the entire prisoner complement gathered in the prison square to witness his punishment for desertion. After a severe beating, he was dragged away unconscious. That was the last we saw of him. The other so-called bad prisoners also were punished before us. They were an Italian and a huge German. Both were beaten and had the bottoms of their bare feet whipped with a rod. The pair whimpered the entire night.

After a few days my spirit was pretty well broken, even though the treatment was eased up a bit, and the food improved slightly. I was relieved from running around the track with the log, and assigned to corveés. Most of these consisted of cleaning out houses. There was no running water, of course, and prisoners were forced to scoop out the mess with their bare hands. We were constantly abused, insulted, kicked, struck, and reminded that we were the lowest of low.

My most bitter memory was Christmas Day 1956 in the Mascara prison. I was in my dungeon cell and the weather was damp and cold. Peering through the overhead bars I could see the rain. Christmas carols floated through the cell window from the rest of the post, and over the walls from the civilians of Mascara. Peace on earth and good will toward men became a hollow mockery. The Turk made his appearance that Christmas Day. He came into my cell and ordered me to my feet.

"Joyeux Noel, Reynolds," he smirked. Before I could answer, his ham of a fist shot out and caught me square on the chin. I stayed on the cement floor looking up at the laughing mad man while he finished up with a couple kicks in the ribs.

By the end of my thirty days I was pretty well broken in spirit, but I still had a vision of escaping. My reactions had become those of a robot. Finally, they issued me different clothing, gave me back my shoelaces, and a most welcome shower. I was being released from prison for transfer back to my company in the other fort in Mascara.

I emerged from the prison fort scarred externally and internally. My mind was haunted by memories of continually running, undergoing beatings, and having close brushes with death. I was marched back to my sleeping quarters and found that my outfit was away on a long march. Until their return I was assigned to work details. When they got back we finished our training at Mascara. I did not have to make up training missed during my month in prison. A friendly lieutenant, who at one time studied at Columbia University, fixed it so that I could move on with my group. Our infantry training was ended, and we were trucked back to the headquarters of the Legion at Sidi Bel Abbes.

CHAPTER 11

I resolved to be the best damned Legionnaire at Bel Abbes. I was determined to do anything to avoid another prison sentence. I also made a vow to escape. My next bid for freedom would have to be successful, either in victory or death. I would never be captured alive. That was my resolution in the new year of 1957.

My next assignment was to the *Escadron,* or cavalry. However, instead of horses or camels, we rode armored vehicles. My tour of duty at Bel Abbes consisted of guard duty at the fort, plus tedious work details and many hours of instructions in the maintenance and operations of vehicles. If we had any strength left at the end of the day we went out on pass in the Legion capital. Nearby was the Casbah, and also *La Negre Ville,* or bordello strip. Churches were scarce. In all my Legion life one great deprivation was the lack of the opportunity to worship. My theory was that the French officers considered a Legionnaire a dog, and dogs don't go to church. I do know that most of the cadres of the Legion are lost souls. Most of them never even received mail, except a small amount at Christmas.

My good comrade Carlos was also assigned to Bel Abbes while I was in training, and he did much to keep my spirits up. His big brother relationship kept me from going the way of so many Legionnaires. Every few weeks one of the poor slobs would go completely nutty. Le Cafard, translated, means the beetle. I have seen several of my comrades grab their heads and scream that the beetles were eating away at their brains. The poor devils were carried away in strait jackets to a rest camp. I never saw any of them again. I know of several who took their lives while in such a state of frenzy. They made good their escape from the Legion of the damned. It was during one of these most depressing periods that Carlos helped me keep my sanity. Unknown to me, he had written to my sister, cautioning my family to help keep my spirits up. In January, 1957, Carlos wrote:

My Dear Sue,

I am a friend of Ronnie's, I suppose the only one in this bad lot. After seeing your photo, I picked up my pen without delay. I have been waiting for the moment when I could sit and think and write about matters that would be interesting both ways, but the time has not yet arrived. If I write to you now, during my ten-minute break, it is to advise you not to write to Ronnie anything that might rise in him the desire to go back home. Not yet, at least. He already made a mistake in that way, and is now paying the consequences. So, for his own good, you must encourage him to stay here, and make the best out of it. Physically he is fine, strong as a bull. Only his morale needs building up. Anyhow, please don't let Ronnie know anything about what I wrote about him. I beg your pardon for my writing, but I am Portuguese, and my English is a bit rusty. Please write to me. It would make me so happy to start a correspondence with you. Soon I will be writing again. Give my best regards to your mother and father and wishing you all the best.

Carlos

Fran Lucca

Shortly after I left the prison at Mascara I wrote to my parents:

Dear Mom and Dad,

I am very sorry that I've not written sooner, but I have been away from the company for a while and it was not possible for me to correspond. If I wrote to you as much as I think of you, Mom and Dad, I would be writing for most of every single day that passes. My mind is at home all the time. only physically and without heart am I here. So please don't believe that my love for you could ever slacken.

I would like to be shoveling snow, painting the house, and washing dishes all the day long if I could have the chance now. When we meet again, Mom and Dad, no matter where, you will understand that no son could have more respect and love for his parents than I have for you. Mom, I can't go to church, but I pray more than ever, and because of the way I have been so very fortunate in different circumstances here, I know that you have been praying much for me. Thank you so, Mom, and you too, Dad. It is very dark in the chamber now. I will try and send this letter by avion.

Legionnaire Reynolds, 114685 and your loving son, sends you his heart.

While at Bel Abbes we went out on a few operations in quest of the Arab partisans. The Fellagha were not then too strong, and carried on a guerrilla type of warfare. Several nights we waited on the cold ground in an attempt to trap some of the N.L.F. No prisoners materialized, for the sly Fellagha avoided our ambushes. I wouldn't be surprised if the Moslem rebels were alerted to the traps by informers right here in Bel Abbes.

I couldn't understand the killing and cruelty. Maybe it was because I felt neutral in the affair. I couldn't see myself shooting at anyone, except at a guy who was aiming a gun at me. But that is all the Legion requires of a man, that idea of self-preservation, combined with the will to defend your comrades. All the Legion had to do was put you in front of enough Arabs that were shooting in your direction, and your natural instincts would have you doing a good job as a soldier.

It was early in April 1957 when the pre-dawn hours came quickly alive with the familiar blast of whistles. It was the call for our assemblement. Another operation was getting under way.

The captain barked, *"Aux armes!"* and dozens of figures sprang to life, jumped into their combat clothes and grabbed their weapons. We lined up outside the fort and presented arms. We marched off in twos into the black and chilly night. We walked to waiting half-tracks and trucks, whose motors were idling with growl-like tones. The whole company was out on this operation. We bounced into a ravine and were halfway across when all hell broke loose -- what seemed like an endless volley of blasts.

"What the hell is going on?" I yelled.

"Ronnie, we have been ambushed! "Carlos called out.

"Where do I shoot?" I asked.

"Get out and take cover behind that mound and keep firing at the top of the ridge," Carlos shouted.

By this time the captain and his sous-officiers had recovered from the initial shock and jumped down from the trucks to assign positions and return the fire. A Greek lad by the name of Markos fell in alongside of me. Carlos was on the other side. Bullets tore the sand and stone in front of me, kicking up a blinding dust. "Keep firing!" screamed the captain, running from man to man as slugs tore into the sand around him. The barrel of my rifle was heating up as it punched out lead. I saw at least a half-dozen robed figures throw up their arms, lean forward, and come tumbling over the crest of the ridge as our bullets found their mark. I was scared, but the excitement helped me overcome my fright somewhat. The turbaned fellagha about fifty yards away started to edge their way toward us. They were about fifteen yards from the top of the ravine when Markos jumped up and fired from the hip. In my frenzy I also leaped to my feet and began pumping away. Carlos freed one arm, and while still in a crouched position slammed his fist into my gut, screaming, "Ronnie, you bleu, keep down!" I doubled up in pain as the breath left me, and found myself choking on a mouthful of sand. The zinging whine of bullets tore inches over me as two rebels found their range. Markos let out an agonizing scream and tumbled on top of me. In the dim light I could see his white face with staring eyes. Blood was trickling from the side of his mouth. As I rolled him off me I felt my hands hot and sticky from his blood. I stared down unbelieving at his still form. A bullet had found its mark in his throat. Carlos was swearing and screaming as his rifle spat out slugs in rapid succession.

When the smoke cleared, the two Arabs were bouncing head over heels down the embankment, out of the battle for good. The captain finally got the situation under control. Riflemen were picking off the fellagha, and the half tracks were swung into position to knock off the nest of rebels. One of the half-tracks swung wildly out of control and came bearing down on Carlos and me. Carlos tripped over some scrub and lay helpless in the path of the rumbling monster. Some superior force moved me with lightning speed. My strength seemed to triple as I reached down and grabbed Carlos under the arms while on the run. Surprisingly, I lifted the rugged Portuguese with ease and dragged him to safety.

"Merci, mon cher ami," smiled Carlos. The only reply I could come up with was, "Carlos, my old friend, I already owe eight of my nine lives to you. I thank God for His assist."

We rushed over to the now halted vehicle to chew out the driver. Karl, a friendly German lad, who couldn't be blamed for the incident. A fantastically lucky shot had sailed through the tiny slit in the front of the half-track to find its mark right between Karl's eyes.

Meanwhile, our captain and a group of men were advancing up the incline and routing N.L.F. Within moments the rebel firing ceased and a small thunder of hoof beats could be heard as they retreated into the hills. The captain called us to assembly and we treated our wounded. Our dead comrades were carried aboard the trucks for burial back at the fort.

Exhausted and somewhat nauseous, I climbed into one of the trucks, sat down, and buried my head in my hands. A strong arm encircled my shoulders and I looked into the grinning face of Carlos, who said proudly, "You came through like a real ancien." A feeling of satisfaction grew within me as we rumbled on through the black night toward the fort. I fell into my bunk completely drained. There was only a little time before Reveille, but I couldn't get right to sleep. I had learned something out there tonight that I never knew existed in the Legion of the damned. I realized that comradeship was a little bit of light that brightened my life here. But a candle was no comparison to the sun. Some misguided souls had joined the Legion for security. For myself, it only made me feel insecure. You didn't even seem to be safe in your own bunk. I had never felt this, even when bumming on the road, when I had the greatest, most wonderful life at all, at home. A soldier must only think of the very present and not wonder a bit about the next hour if he is to be at all content. I was trying to accomplish this state of mind, but it seemed to take a long time. Some of the other men seemed to have this fortunate attitude. I tried to develop it. For example, when I thought of home. I tried to do it without feeling. I'd say to myself, "Home. I love my home. That is where my beloved parents are sleeping now." But time passes. Time always goes on.

At Ghardia desert outpost where Ron trained
to fight the rebels in the mountains.

CHAPTER 12

My next assignment was deep in the Sahara. Apparently the Legion thought this a good place for me because of my previous aborted bid for freedom. It would be far more difficult to escape in the desert. Carlos got an enviable assignment with a northern regiment. I was to miss him greatly. My destination was Company Two, CSPL, at the outpost of Ghardaia, many miles to the south. It was a torturous trip over a lifeless oven of sand and stone. My quarters were in an old stone hospital two stories high, with small windows overlooking the barren no man's land for endless miles. My desert fighting would include several months from the walled Ghardaia outpost. I also spent some time in the slightly more civilized outpost town of Laghouat. These positions were hundreds of miles south of Bel Abbes.

Algeria is a vast country, and not all sandy desert. In 1957 it was a protectorate of France, covering about 850,000 square miles, or almost one-third the area of the continental United States. The population was about ten million. In the north, along the Mediterranean Sea, is an area of fertile plain from fifty to one hundred miles wide. South of the plain is the Atlas mountain chain, reaching to altitudes of seven thousand feet. Further south is the desert. Over ninety percent of the people live in the northern area along the sea. Also, at that time, about ninety percent of the people were Arab, and the rest European. Therefore, in the area south of the mountains there lived about ten percent of the people in about ninety percent of the territory. In the north there is much agriculture, and products including wheat, oats, wine, olive oil, dates and figs. The cities of course, are in the north. The desert area south of the mountains is not flat and sandy, but is hilly and rocky and desolate. The temperature changes radically from stifling heat in the day to freezing cold at night.

When not out on operations seeking the NLF rebels we were kept busy from sunrise to sunset digging wells, building roads, or on numerous corveés. The Legion not only extended the empire of France by fighting, but also built the roads and forts that cemented the empire together. My guess was that the French believed that a tired Legionnaire was a well behaved one. The French also have a rare eye for a franc, and in the Legion they not only found cheap fighting men, but also cheap labor.

My first couple of months were spent at Ghardaia. The area around Ghardaia was most primitive. The old, unfinished hospital, which served as our fort, had incomplete plumbing. It had room for the cots of about half the company, or about fifty men. The main part of the group was in the fort at Houat, several hundred miles away. There were four C.S.P.L. units, with about four hundred men in each unit. Most of the Legionnaires were further north in the infantry regiments, where a larger population brewed more trouble.

Once we stepped outside the walled town there was nothing but miles and miles of expanse and desert. Here on the hot desert sand, our job was to carry on a hit-run guerrilla type warfare with the Arab bands. The NLF did most of the hitting and running, while we in the C.S.P.L took after them like blood hounds and tried to flush them out of their strongholds in the hills. In some cases, Arab towns were wiped out by the rebels because they did not cooperate with the revolt. Secret taxes were levied on towns to support the revolution, under threats of retaliation. The French made great use of this as propaganda in an effort to influence neutral Arabs. The Legion occupied forts in the towns. When information was obtained on the whereabouts of the fellagha, the Legion was alerted. Then the C.S.P.L. moved quickly.

One of several typical operations occurred in mid-July of 1957. We were just finishing our breakfast when the whistle blasts alerted us and the bugle call *"Aux Armes"* sent us scampering for our gear. Diblazi, my Italian copain yelled, "Travel light, Ronnie, you may be marching for a couple of days."

"Don't worry," I replied, "My back is still aching from our last fouage." At that time, I had carried extra clothing and food, and was really weighed down. To make matters worse, I had rubbed the corporal the wrong way, and as a result, he took away my light machine gun, and gave me a sack of ammunition, which weighed about ten kilo, or thirty pounds. In addition, I was lugging a FM machine gun which also weighed thirty pounds, plus my rifle, food, shelter half and personal gear. This time I was dressed in my combat fatigues and leggings. I grabbed my helmet and ammo belt, and got my rifle from the magazine. Diblazi called back to me, "Don't forget your *dishdasha*. It gets very cold out there at night."

I dashed back into the chamber for the long flowing Arab robe. These robes had an attached cowl which could be pulled over the head. I had learned to value my dishdasha highly. Enroute to the waiting trucks I grabbed a handful of C rations from the commissary.

About fifteen trucks were waiting to begin our operations, and I fell in next to Diblazi beside the lead truck. Sharp looking and battle wise Captain Plantivan came along with two of his aides. We stood at attention while the captain reviewed us and checked our arms.

"*Alors!*" he shouted, and we climbed aboard for the lengthy ride to the base of the hills in which the wily rebels were. For three hours the trucks rumbled over the rough roads, leaving a trail of dust that seemed to hang in space. The mountains loomed closer. We had climbed as high as we could in the trucks, and the single lane dirt track had finally come to an end on a knoll of wild vegetation and scrub trees. A sergeant-chef jumped from the lead half-track and signaled the convoy into a semi-circle formation. We jumped down and gathered our equipment. Captain Plantivan gave us a final briefing. The helicopters would arrive soon to take us up into the mountains where the NLF were last sighted. Eduardo, a Spaniard, who was a veteran of seven years in the Legion, took me aside.

"Ron, stick with me and you will be alright," he said. "Remember, we take no prisoners."

"All I want to do is get this damn operation over with and get back to the fort," I replied. Diblazi laughed.

"Keep alert, friend, or you will be carried back in a sack."

"Don't worry," I answered, "this kid will take care of himself."

The noise of motors caught our attention and we glanced up to see five Sikorsky choppers floating into our area. The whirlybirds touched down in the middle of our half-circle and the rotating blades came to a halt. When the sand and dust settled, we were marched aboard the choppers. Then it was up and away over the hills. About fifteen minutes later the choppers glided toward a partially level plateau and began their descent. We were hovering about three feet from the ground when our crew leader jumped up and shouted, "All right men, out you go!"

I was fifth in line. Eduardo was first. He stepped into space and a shot rang out from the brush. Almost simultaneously there was a scream from Eduardo that died on his lips. He was dead before he hit the ground, a bullet through his chest. More gunfire came from the brush and slugs were tearing into the chopper.

"Keep moving," screamed the sergeant as he pushed us from the helicopter. The whine of bullets chilled me. I said a quick prayer, ran to the open door and leaped out. I held my breath, half expecting a bullet to greet me. The next instant, I was on the ground eating dirt. Before I could rollout of the way a screaming figure landed on top of me. It was the big red-headed Scotchman. He never had a chance. A bullet had entered his right cheek and ·torn upward through his helmet. I pushed his lifeless form aside and dashed into the bushes. I jerked the helmet up from in front of my eyes and began firing blindly into the foliage.

Other Legionnaires were getting into position and there was heavy firing for a few minutes. Then a whistle blew and the captain called a halt. We were quickly assembled and a count was taken. Four of the Legionnaire raiders in my Sikorsky would never see Bel Abbes again. At least a dozen others from the other choppers also suffered fatal wounds in the brief encounter. Close to two dozen Arabs had been killed in the skirmish. Our platoon leader took us aside and formed us into a single file for the trek up the paths in pursuit of the rebels. The captain came over and motioned to me. I was given the job of moving in advance of the company to scout. The region was totally strange to me, but as familiar to the Arabs as the backs of their hands.

One consolation, however, was the fact that Abdul, an Arab scout for the Legion, would be close by. He was an eerie looking devil, with his beady eyes, scraggly beard, and filthy turban and robe. In addition to his rifle and ammo belt, he carried a wicked looking knife which was stained with the blood of some of his rebel countrymen.

I was about fifty yards in front of our group. It felt like I was alone, except for the unseen enemy. I was made no happier by the realization that one of my duties was to draw enemy fire. Often the rebels allowed the scouts to pass unharmed, saving their surprise attack for the main body. Even if that happened, I was still in a bad spot. To add to our misery, a sudden downpour soaked us to the skin and slowed us down. After several hours, darkness closed in like a mantle of death. We made camp for the night near a ravine.

Suddenly several bullets tore into our midst. "Hit the ground and take cover!" shouted the captain. Lead kicked up stones and dirt, and a volley of shots deafened us to the command of our leaders. The hand signals of a grizzled sergeant directed us to a vantage point, where we could return the fire of the rebels who were holed up in grotto-like caves. The shooting continued throughout the night.

When dawn finally broke I saw a bundle of clothing a few feet away. It turned out to be the headless body of my friend Francesco. The Spanish teenager who joined the Legion to fight, had just completed his first and last battle. One of the Arabs had crawled down to our position and beheaded the unsuspecting Francesco. By a stroke of fate my comrade in arms a short distance away was the victim of the sneak attack. I had never realized a fanatical Arab rebel was so close to me. Instead of instilling me with fear, I was infuriated, and vowed to kill every Arab I could.

As I maintained my position awaiting the word to proceed with the attack I kept thinking of the bundle of flesh and clothing within my view. I had plenty of time to do a lot of thinking during that long and weary night, waiting for daybreak and the advance on the enemy. I wondered why I, an American, was involved in this mess of killing. The French made no secret of the fact that they were contemptuous of Americans. They thought America was foolish to give weapons to a foreign country. That did not make them hesitate to use weapons supplied by NATO. As I lay on the chilly ground, I realized that the French had a good thing in the Legion. They didn't have to use their own men and didn't even use their own weapons. The French used the bastards of the world to help in acquiring colonies, and in keeping the natives subjugated. France did not have to lose any of her men, except for a few French officers who were killed while serving with the Legion. Most of the dying was done by the enlisted mercenaries from dozens of nations. The French army didn't get into combat except by accident. They had a fort next to ours, but the troops never seemed to go out on operations. In their regular army fort they had about three or four hundred men, but for garrison duty only. The French regulars did not hesitate to pass on the dirty details to us. They didn't seem to care what happened to Algeria. Most of them were draftees. However, I must give due credit to the French regular paratroopers. They were the only active French units.

The conduct of France in the Indochina war was lackadaisical. Most of the fighting was done by the foreigners of the Legion. By the end of the hostilities in 1954, the United States was supplying seventy-five percent of the weapons and equipment. In spite of all this, France lost the colonies, and then, to top it all off, many of the French blamed the U.S. for their loss. They had raised the spectre of communism and the United States had responded. But still France lost out. What would the outcome be in Algeria? It was no secret that France played a cynical game in Indochina, to hold on to a colony which it had been exploiting for a century. France used foreigners to do its fighting and the United States furnished the supplies. Sure, the war was mostly a battle for freedom by the natives, but the United States was led to believe that this was part of the world-wide struggle against communism. For this reason, Uncle Sam was willing to furnish the supplies. The French were glad to act as the middleman and pass these items onto the Legion, which was exposed to all the bloodshed.

There was a rather similar situation in Algeria. France had held Algeria for a century and a quarter, mainly through the efforts of the Legion. The native Arabs of Algeria wanted their freedom, but the French were using us in the Legion to hold on to the area. France was more or less blackmailing the U.S. into supporting its stand in Algeria. DeGaulle was threatening to have France quit the United Nations if the U.S. did not use its power to block a U.N. discussion on the Algerian situation. Once again France was attempting to frighten the United States with charges of the success of communism, or of Russian expansion.

In the morning we edged closer to the caves and made our final assault. We were moving in a fan formation through the rough terrain. The lead scouts were many yards ahead and completely out of my sight. I was about fifty yards in front of the main group, as lead man. Chunks of stones splattered me as rebel fire from the grottos pecked away at the walls bordering the narrow ravine through which I tramped. The going became so rough that we were ordered into single file. The firing became much heavier and bullets were kicking up stones and dirt all around. The company hit the dust and poured round after round of ammunition into the caves, but the rebel fire did not let up. The captain hastily summoned his squad leaders and within moments a sergeant tapped me on the shoulder and motioned me over to the side of the trail, where about a dozen other men had been assembled. The sergeant said, "You men will crawl to within throwing distance and flush out the salauds with hand grenades. Good luck."

I ran in a crouching position as near as I dared to the rebel infested caves. There were four grottos to take care of. Part of the patrol already was lobbing the grenades into the openings. Within a half-hour, three of the grottos were stilled, but the fourth cave was still active. It was at an awkward angle, and our grenades were unable to flush out the NLF. Finally Captain Plantivan called to Mario, a veteran survivor of the Dien Bien Phu slaughter in 1954. Mario at one time had performed on the highwire with his circus family in Italy. I couldn't imagine what the two were talking about. The captain was pointing to the rebel held grotto and Mario was nodding his head in agreement. Then he dashed off to the left of the cave and began scaling the rocky hill.

We were ordered to cease fire while Mario was on his mission. The NLF kept up their sniping, but found few targets. After a few minutes, I could see Mario scampering to a point about twenty feet above the cave's opening. Then he took one end of a line from around his waist and secured it to a large boulder directly over the cave. Mario pulled the line taut and started lowering himself toward the top of the opening. Undetected by the rebels, the wiry Legionnaire halted his descent just above the grotto so that his dangling legs wouldn't be seen. Then in a maneuver familiar to aerialists, he kicked up his legs and wrapped them around the line over his head. The next second Mario was swinging head down, tossing a deadly grenade into the cave. He pulled himself into a safe position just before the blast. The shooting from the grotto was stilled, and within minutes, so were the agonizing screams.

Our mission was completed. However, a day's march would be needed for the rendezvous with our helicopters. They would be waiting for us part way down the mountain for our return trip to the trucks standing by. First came more important duties, such as burying our dead. The fellaghas, dressed in their robes, pantaloons, and turbans, were left for the buzzards.

The Fellagha {FLN} were usually found in grotto type caves and had to be flushed or burned out like animals.

Legionnaires bury one of their own following a raid against FLN rebels in mountains near the outpost of Laghuat in the Sahara.

Captain Plantivan..tough but fair, calls his troops to arms for a helicopter operation into the hills to flush out the FLN.

Few of the Fellagha are taken prisoners. They are usually killed after questioning. The Legion doesn't bury them. They leave them for the buzzards.

The Legionnaires scurry for cover after landing in the desert for a raid against Algerian rebels.

An Arab guide on the operation was indispensable because the enemy knew the terrain well. But he feared capture by the FLN.

CHAPTER 13

The return to the helicopters was delayed for another day while we looked for more rebels in the area. Food and ammunition were parachuted to us. We had a couple of minor skirmishes, but had done about what we could to secure the region. Another problem was interrogating the few prisoners we had taken in hopes of learning the whereabouts of large groups of rebels.

I was ordered to help escort the wretched rebel prisoners to the rendezvous area. Some were bleeding from their unattended wounds. I reached out to try to help one of the rebels who had a steady flow of blood from his shoulder. Heinrich, the brutal assistant squad leader, nearly broke my arm with a judo slash.

"Dammit it all, Heinrich," I snapped, "what did you do that for?"

"Reynolds, it is best that you go over to the pick-up area and wait. Our business here won't be long. We have ways of dealing with our prisoners which you queasy Americans cannot stomach."

I didn't argue. I walked over to the other group, but picked a spot where I could observe what was happening. It was then that I got another shock, which left me with a new source of nightmares, and a rededicated vow to escape. In spite of all I had seen and heard before, it was difficult for me now to believe my eyes.

A Legion lieutenant had summoned his special contingent of persuaders to torture the rebels for information of other NLF strongholds. The methods used were savage. One of the Moslems was strung up by his toes, his head a few inches above the ground. After a half hour of flogging, he talked. Nearby was a large tub of water and a gasoline operated pump. Attached to the pump was a hose. I stared with shock as one end of the hose was rammed up the rear of a screaming rebel. Water was pumped into him until he became bloated. Then the interrogator stomped on his stomach until excretion poured from his mouth, drowning out his agonizing screams.

Two ex-Nazi storm troopers of NCO rank took pride in the wiring job they did on an Arab's privates. After the electrical charge the prisoner fell to the ground in a babbling heap. A French colon of captain rank in the gendarmes was the most atrocious. I stared in horror as he swung a cleaver down on a screaming prisoner's finger. I turned away sick to my stomach as the captain continued his gruesome work, taking one finger at a time. The rest of the prisoners had pointed sticks jammed under their fingernails and ignited. They talked freely before passing out from the pain.

We were ordered aboard the Sikorsky bananas for our return trip to the trucks.

"What about the prisoners?" I asked a noncom.

"Don't worry about them. They will meet their *Allah* very shortly," he replied grimly.

I heard a volley of shots and dying screams. The questioning was over and the examiners picked up their equipment and headed for the helicopters. Needless to say there were no prisoners for the return trip. I was silent during the flight back to the trucks. Most of the other men also were quiet. Only Heinrich and one of his old Nazi cohorts found much to chuckle about.

What had I become a part of? Deep inside, my sympathies were with the Arabs. I couldn't blame the Arabs for wanting the French out of Algeria. I knew that most of the Legionnaires never cared for the French cause. We were just doing our duty to pass away the years of enlistment. Practically every Legionnaire hated the French officers, but he would never reveal this fact. Our only cause for fighting was the fact that we were

Legionnaires. We fought for the Legion. A Legionnaire is proud in a defiant manner. We in the Legion were superior fighting men, and we knew it. It was the only way in which we were outstanding. We had a reckless, starved life, and believed we had nothing to lose. A Legionnaire is imbued with the idea of living for the moment, catching what little pleasure he can. And his only fear is Legion discipline. The sous-officiers treated us better while on fouage because they knew that if they acted toward us out here as they did at the fort, their lives wouldn't be worth much. Actually I hated my sous-officiers more than an fellagha. But what could you do about it in the Legion? I wouldn't care if France lost the whole of Algeria. My real regret was that America had helped these people so much. In my opinion, the French were the most insecure, unprincipled people that could exist. And yet, on the surface, they pretended to be the smiling friends of the U.S. I wished that officials in Washington could change places with me for a few days and become more enlightened on French politics. Some Americans seem to feel that we must go to any lengths to keep France on our side. These people claimed that France was a powerful ally with a major NATO base in Western Europe. In actuality, France had received much aid from Uncle Sam to help defend Europe, but diverted much of this material to Africa, where it was used against the natives. To some extent, American manpower was defending France while Frenchmen were used to occupy

North Africa. The preoccupation of France with Algeria greatly reduced its effectiveness as a member of NATO. This forced the United States to rely more on West Germany. And this in turn frightened the Russians, who became more belligerent and continued the vicious circle.

It is possible that American support of freedom would alienate France temporarily, but in the long run it would have to be friendly. This would mean that the United States was living up to its ideal of freedom. The U.S. has a propaganda weapon far more powerful than that of the Communist. Both the U.S. and the U.S.S.R. claim they are for freedom. Russia asserts it is for economic freedom and against colonialism. The Russians have nothing to lose by such talk, and much to gain in power throughout Asia and Africa. The unschooled multitudes of these two continents have shown much interest in Russia's claims. Some of these listeners have the opinion that the U.S. is hypocritical in talking freedom, but acting in support of colonial power.

However, these were distant problems, and I had a more immediate and serious one. Freedom was being denied to me by the French Foreign Legion. It was true that men joined of their own free will, and so had I. I knew that armies could not allow their members the degree of freedom that civilians had. I doubt that any man who joined the Legion for the first time had any conception of the military straitjacket or horrible prison-type existence he was entering. Few Americans join the Legion, and we are shocked because it is such a contrast to our former freedom and prosperity.

As the helicopter began its descent near the circle of trucks I thought once again of the bundles of flesh and clothing left behind. Only yesterday those poor souls were pulsating personalities. A live Legionnaire wasn't too much better off. The trip back to the fort was uneventful. I went straight to my chamber and plopped on my bunk fully clothed, ammunition belt and all. I fell asleep instantly.

We spent two months at Ghardaia and then switched our operations to Laghouat. It was quite a contrast from the walled town of Ghardaia, which in turn is about fifteen hundred miles south of Sidi Bel Abbes. The route into Ghardaia was by train, going from Bel Abbes to Bida, on to Algiers, and then south to Djelfa. Then it was straight south to Laghouat, and finally by truck the rest of the way to Ghardaia. When we had come from Bel Abbes it had taken three days. Ghardaia was very primitive. Once you stepped outside the walls there was nothing but miles of desert. Except for the soldiers, the people were all Arabs. In Laghouat there were Europeans, tiny shops, and bordellos. We had liberty most nights, but our money usually ran out the first liberty after payday.

We were quick to investigate the bordellos of Laghouat. They contained no beds, but only cots and quilts on the earthen floor. Many of them were off limits because of disease. There was quite a contrast in the bordello of this southern area with those of the more populated north. In the desert the pay for play girls only provided a covering on a caked mud floor. The north was more stylish. In Bel Abbes there were large houses. The madame was usually a squat, middle-aged woman in a tight-fitting black silk dress that revealed an overflow of fat, sloppy breasts, and noticeable bulges fore and fat below her mid-section. Cash on the line was the first order of business. Inside the spacious first story you would find numerous customers seated on a bench that went along three sides of the room. A cloud of cheap perfume hung over the area. A stairway led to an open inside balcony which had access to about a dozen doors. Periodically, a woman of southern European or Arabic origin would appear on the balcony, open her kimono to the sex starved customers below and tease coyly, "Zigi Zigi, mon cherie." Then she would be joined by a half dozen ladies of joy, and they would parade down the stairs to give customers their choice. After feeling the merchandise, the customer would climb the staircase with his choice and enter one of the rooms. It would be plain with bare walls and empty of furniture, except for a cot. Next to the cot was a basin of water and a cloth. Often the slop bucket wasn't emptied until a dozen or so of spent customers were drained. The action was over quickly, and the satisfied patron was hurried out to the accompaniment of *"Vite! Vite!"* As a man vacated the room, another customer was hurried inside. Business was on an assembly line basis. The cots never cooled down.

In the north they also had the B.M.C. or *Bordel Mobile de Companie,* which was a cat house on wheels. These prostitutes were sponsored by the Legion. They set up their flesh shops in a corner room of the caserne, which was usually kept vacant in anticipation of the infrequent visits of the traveling trollops. It was a seller's market. These mobile love factories had such enticing names as *"La Lune"* (The Moon) and *"La Soleil"* (The Sun). Barbed wire was usually strung around the concubine compound, not to keep out the customers, but to funnel them through a checkpoint. A soldier had to get a military pass to visit a *bordel militare.* He handed this pass to a corporal when entering the red light area. At this time, he was given a hurried inspection for venereal disease. Then his name was entered into a notebook. If this man later was afflicted by a social disease, he would be treated in the Legion infirmary. If his name was not in the book and he picked up a dose, he would be punished. There were many Arab bordellos around, but these were out of bounds because of the prevalence of disease. In the desert to the south, the mobile Arab prostitutes set up their tents outside the fort every payday. Their operation usually lasted a couple of days, because after that the Legionnaires were broke. Then the caravan would pull up stakes and move on to its next stop. Many of the women were part Arab and part European. Those of pure European descent were mostly older rejects from the continent of Europe. When they got too old to turn a decent trick in Europe they would go to Africa, where men could not afford to be so fussy.

CHAPTER 14

When not on furlough some of the men read books they were able to scrounge. I spent some time reading by candle light, but this usually got me down in the dumps, because it reminded me of all that I was missing. I used my rare spare moments studying French from books my parents sent me. If I had a few odd francs, I could go to the *foyer,* or canteen, and buy cans of food such as beans or sugared condensed milk. The canned milk stilled my hunger and fulfilled the need for sweets, although I never touched such a thing back home. We also could buy beer and cigarettes. I didn't smoke, but I could swap my cigarettes for anything my Legionnaire comrades might have.

It was one of those lonely nights that my thoughts drifted back to Buffalo and my wonderful grandparents. There was still an hour before lights out, so I decided to drop them a line and explain my situation.

Dear Gram and Pa,

At last I write you and send you my love. Yes, I have come to the French Foreign Legion and I can hardly believe it myself. All I can do now is ask your forgiveness. You gave me a wonderful life those years that I spent with you, and you always gave me the best advice and guidance. When I listened to you I became a success in school and in sports. Even when I only half listened to you and Mom and Dad, I still had a good life and I got over the hurdles. But I closed my ears to all and took off for Florida and then to Europe to travel the roads to nowhere. Now, and only now, I realize that all I have been looking and searching for was what I left at home. I had escaped to nowhere. I realize now that at home is the love that all men search for. Because I was foolish and didn't listen to you, the refusal from the Florida college made me blindly mad and completely deaf to good words of guidance. One thing about the Legion is that it lets a man see all the mistakes of his past life as if they were taking place right before him at the moment.

What is done is done, and I just want to thank you with my whole heart for the wonders of happiness you gave me in the past life, Gram and Pa. No boy could have been treated with greater kindness and love. Mom and Dad wrote me of the merry Christmas you all had at home. I was really cheered to hear of that. Gram and Pa, I really would be pleased if you could send me a picture of yourselves.

Well, goodbye for now Gram and Pa. Please don't think that because I have not written you before, that I do not think of you all the time, every day. I pray for your happiness every night Gram and Pa.

Your loving Grandson,
Ronnie

During my first break the following day I decided on a chore that was quite infrequent -- doing my laundry. This took much time because I had to guard my clothes while they were drying, or else they would be stolen.

Sometimes more than a hundred soldiers would do their washing in the same water. The soap we were issued was almost impossible. If I had a few extra francs, I would purchase a better soap called "Omo" at the foyer. If I couldn't afford the Omo I would have to use the strong bars of yellow soap. After scrubbing my clothes in the cold water in the eight-foot trough, I would have to rinse them in the same water. I never saw hot water in the Legion. However, often I was out on a work detail at shower time, so I actually averaged a shower every two weeks.

I pulled guard duty one dreary night and had an acute attack of depression. The prospect of four more years of hell before discharge. My first furlough couldn't come until after three and a half years in the Legion. Even that wasn't much of a treat because it had to be spent at the Legion depot at Arzew in northern Algeria, and was filled with roll calls, guard duties, and corveés. My mind kept turning to my abortive attempt to escape, and it was difficult to visualize ever getting away. I felt that I was reaching the end of the line. I began to become fascinated by the razor sharp bayonet on the end of my rifle. Something came over me and I wedged the rifle into the ground at the stock, and stared at the shining blade of destruction. All I had to do was fall forward on the point, and it would be all over. My escape from the Legion of lost souls would be accomplished. The sparkling death tip of my rifle was hypnotic, and I began to sway dizzily toward the instrument of death. Somewhere in the past I saw Danke, a handsome blond Swede who was in my billet in Mascara. I could see him at the ammo depot with a machine gun pressed to his stomach. I also saw several of his copains rushing to him, and then stopping in their tracks as the ear splitting tattoo of bullets ended his Legion career by spreading his guts all over the wall behind him. I found myself reciting a short prayer learned from the good sisters during catechism instructions while only a boy. Then I steadied myself, shook my head, and removed the rifle from its suicidal position. I dropped to my knees and asked God for His forgiveness for my weak moment of despair. I began to hope that faith and prayers would see me through somehow. I vowed then and there that if I did get home again, I would do all within my power to live up to His expectations.

After a rough two additional weeks of sporadic skirmishes in the hills, the NLF finally let up and we were able to enjoy a day's pass. A few hours outside the post was a rare treat. The twelve-foot high iron gate swings open and a different world unfolds. A short distance away the windowless stucco houses of the Arabs can be seen. Narrow, hard mud streets wind through the town. The life of the community is spent outdoors, mostly in hollowed rectangular courtyards. The bigger streets have narrow walks clinging to the one story houses. There are no cars, just donkeys, burros, and a few dogs and cats. The natives seem lazy and disorganized in their cluttered living. In the middle of the town is a pyramid nestled on a tiny knoll. In the center of the pyramid, pointing straight up like the top of a Christmas tree, is a minaret. As you neared the middle of the town, you could hear chanting from the gathering of people near the minaret. Next to a square, evidently set up by the Europeans, there were benches, a scattering of palm trees, and lonely clumps of grass. And there was the inevitable statue of a French officer of past glory. Spotted around the square were little shops and tiny cafes. A cafe would have a few chairs out front, and a table or two. The Arabs seemed content to sit on the ground under a tree. Some were dressed in their shoulder to ankle burnooses, or in oversized bloomer-type pants. Others wore cast off European clothing. There were several Arab shops looking like ancient second-hand stores, and few better European shops. Arabs would bicker at length before a purchase was consummated.

Once you had seen the *kasbah,* or native section, of any Algerian town, you had seen them all. In the Arab home the front door was usually a blanket. Inside the one-room hut there was straw covering the mud floor. Chickens, goats, and other small animals shared the cramped quarters. There were no toilet facilities. The natives just did as the animals did. Some of the Arabs had an elevated bed with rags for blankets. Most of the cooking was done outdoors. The fuel was wood that came from something that looked like a big weed. The aroma of an Arab home was unforgettable. It was a mixture of sweet smelling oil and manure.

After sightseeing I returned to the post and was happy to be surprised by a letter and package from my parents. I replied.

Dear Mom and Dad,

I sure am a lucky guy. Your ingenuity in packing my present was marvelous. I am now brushing my teeth with bubbly Crest, having some delicious stuffed dates with my coffee, enjoying the tasty quality of our American candy after dinner, and generally feeling great with everything I touch that came from your hands and through your loving hearts. It was an especially fine thought to send the cigarettes too, for the guys here really get a kick out of smoking the rare and superior American brands. Everything coming from our factories, farms, and export houses, is by far the best quality in the world. For example, I have eaten many dates since I have been in Africa, but never those to even compare in taste to the ones you sent me. Another thing, for the candy covered almonds that cost twenty-nine cents, I would pay three hundred francs for here. That would equal about eighty cents, or one and one-half days' wages for a Legionnaire. We earn about seven thousand francs per month now. Three hundred and fifty francs equal one dollar, so we get twenty dollars a month, or sixty-five cents a day. Here, wages are low, and prices high, and they have the poverty to show for it.

I am now deep in the Sahara with the C.S.P.L. Companie Saharienne Portee Legion. There is nothing here. The sun burns up a heat as you can never experience in America. Whichever way you turn there are stony hills, sand and desert. We are now stationed in a small oasis village. There are palms, but they extend only a few yards outside town. If you can try and imagine this, as you are driving through our beautifully tree-strewn city, and then realize how wonderful it is in Buffalo.

Miss you very much as always, Mom and Dad. I think of you all the time. Out here a guy does nothing but think. Always thought about things too much, but it is too late to change now. What I try to do is sleep as much as possible.

What are our papers saying about the North African situation? Are we helping France? I hope not. Are we giving arms to Morocco and Tunisia? I'm hoping the enemy will grow stronger and stronger. I told you I prefer the Arabs to the French.

Your letter was so warming, Mom. It was fine of you to write before you went to sleep that night past. Thank you for all of your prayers. I hope that you and Dad had a pleasant time in D.C. and that the monument for our Mother Mary is constructed in accordance to the beauty and grandeur that she deserved. Goodbye for now.

Your loving son,
Ronnie

The next morning the corporal pulled me from a work detail.

"Reynolds, to the captain's office suite. An American bigshot to see you."

"Don't tell me Washington is finally going to get me out of this hell hole," I replied.

The corporal glared at me and snarled, "'The only way you will leave us, Reynolds, is in a pine box."

"Blow it out, *saloud*," I muttered, as I headed for the captain's office.

"Come in Reynolds," called out the captain. "This is Mr. Ainsworth from the American consulate in Algiers."

"How do you do, sir," I responded.

"Hello, Reynolds, I've stopped by to do some checking on you. Your parents have been in contact with Washington in hopes of having you released from the Legion on the grounds that you were underage when you enlisted. However, I'm sorry to inform you that those grounds for appeal are lacking. I also have the duty to inform you that according to the law as of 1952, because you have joined a foreign army, you have lost your citizenship."

I stared at him in disbelief and shock. "My God, Mr. Ainsworth, I never counted on that. Isn't there something you can do? It's true, I joined the Legion voluntarily, but they never told me I would lose my citizenship."

The French officers talked nervously and looked at one another. They were careful not to leave the room, and never allowed me to talk to Ainsworth privately. The captain spoke up, "I'm sure, Consul, that our recruiting officer made all these specifications quite clear. Why, we even send a recruit away for twenty-four hours to make up his mind before he signs up."

"Sir, I would gladly accept repatriation," I appealed to Ainsworth.

"I'm sorry, Reynolds, but that is not possible. We sympathize with you, and promise to look further into your case. I already have urged the French government to release you as a matter of simple justice, and as a move to help strengthen the friendly relations between France and the United States. I make no pledges, but I will try to be helpful."

And that was it. I was dismissed and went back to my corveé. Extreme depression swept over me. It seemed certain now that the only way out of the Legion was to escape. The bitter memory of my first futile attempt was still with me, but while standing guard duty that night, my thoughts returned again and again to how I could escape. Escape was in the minds of most of the Legionnaires. They talked about it a great deal, but only to intimate friends. If they trusted their listener, escape talk took up half the conversation. Many of the Legionnaires were afraid to actually make a move because of the heavy odds against them. In spite of this, quite a number did try to get away. With me, escape was becoming an obsession. It always was on my mind. Besides my one aborted attempt there would be two more tries that never materialized. They had collapsed before they were actually put into motion. I realized that if I were ever caught again it might mean my life. The probable sentence would be two years in the dreaded Colomb-Bechar, the devil's island of the desert. This was the final penal camp for the Legion and few men survived it. And those that did lost much of their sanity. I felt deeply that I would rather be killed trying to escape than resign myself to trying to serve out my full five-year enlistment. There was a possibility I wouldn't live that long, anyhow, and I preferred to die as an escapee under my own will.

CHAPTER 15

The agonizing months of desert duty began to take their toll. I felt myself getting weaker, and noticed that my weight was dropping. The climax came one afternoon while with the second cavalry. I felt worse than usual and tried to alleviate this by extra helpings of wine in addition to the usual portion of pinard. We were on an operation in the sand dunes. My head was splitting and I thought it was a reaction to the wine. We were enroute back to the fort in trucks, and every time we would hit a rut, pain flashed through my head. Then I started to get sick to my stomach. A sergeant-chef by the name of Amanti came over to me.

"What is it private? Nausea?"

I felt so bad that I snarled, "Feel sick, hell! I am sick. Damned sick! I'm sick of the Legion, sick of France, sick of the Arabs, and sick of every one of you!" My head felt like a hot poker. Another non-com came over, and I expected a boot in the face. It was the sadistic Heinrich.

"*Was fehlt ihm?*" he snarled.

"What the hell is he saying, Amanti?" I asked.

Amanti took it from there. "He is a sick one, Heinrich, and should be doctored." Heinrich only grunted his dissatisfaction and crawled back to his seat in the truck. Amanti helped me off the truck and was walking me to my bedchamber when Heinrich came over and ordered me to stand guard duty.

"He is *umbriago*," bellowed Heinreich, "and shall stand his post."

"You blasted Kraut!" I shouted. "I am not drunk."

Heinrich was about to belt me when a lieutenant was attracted by the commotion and came over. Sergeant Amanti came to my rescue.

"This man is very sick, lieutenant. and should not be allowed to stand guard." The officer touched my head. I knew I was feverish, but when the lieutenant ordered the noncom to relieve me of guard duty I felt indebted to the officer. I hit the sack without supper, but when I awakened the next morning, I felt worse than ever. It seemed as though someone was pounding my head with a sledgehammer, and I knew that I couldn't hold anything on my stomach. The last thing I wanted was an operation in the mountains, and this was what was called for. The trip in the truck to the helicopter was hell. I couldn't keep my head up.

When we arrived I was barely able to climb out of the vehicle. We waited a day and a half in bivouac before the Sikorskys arrived. I stumbled to my assigned chopper and struggled aboard. The way I felt I would just as soon stand in the line of fellagha fire. Then my misery would be ended. I prayed for some miracle to halt the operation.

Almost unreal, it happened. My helicopter developed engine trouble and the whole operation was scrubbed. Then it was back to the fort in the jolting truck. As I climbed from the truck, I collapsed. When I awakened I was in a strange place, for a Legionnaire. The room was an immaculate white and I was lying on a soft mattress between clean sheets for the first time since my Legion enlistment. A smiling French doctor was at my bedside.

"Was I here all night?" I asked. "What's wrong with me?"

"You, soldier, are a victim of yellow jaundice, with complications, including dysentery."

"Where am I?"

"Not far from your fort. In fact, just next to it. This is the French regular army caserne, and you are in our infirmary. The Legion has no doctors, so we French regulars take over when one of the Legionnaires becomes ill."

"Thank God for that," I mumbled under my breath. For the first time in my Legion hitch I was to be treated like a human being. For the next month I would get nothing but fine care and delicious food like meat, milk and vegetables, and clean quarters. As for medication, there was none for jaundice. Just rest and greaseless food.

I made another promise to myself--my fighting career in the Legion was over. I wonder what my fate would have been if the balky helicopter had taken off and gone into the mountains. It is very possible that I would not have returned alive.

Babette, the lovely nurse assigned to my ward was like a breath of spring whenever she was nearby. She read to me in French and kept after me to write home. Babette was not much older than me, but her eyes indicated that she had seen too much for her age. One day I finally got up the courage to ask, "Tell me Babette, why such a lovely young woman as yourself has not a wedding band to go with the diamond engagement ring?" She stiffened suddenly, and her eyes became moist. She was about to leave, when she stopped short, and in a quivering voice replied, "If you would have taken notice, you would have seen that the ring is on my right hand."

"I'm sorry, Babette, I didn't think."

"That's alright, soldier. I don't mind telling you. My heart is buried fifty miles south of the Chinese border in a valley high in the Thai Mountains, in a place called Dien Bien Phu."

"Forgive me, Babette. It was thoughtless of me. Could you tell me about him?"

"His name was Niles, and he was from a little town outside of Rotterdam. We met in Marseilles while I was in training. He had only one more year to serve with la Légion étrangère when war came to Dien Bien Phu in 1954."

"What outfit was he with?"

"Niles was with the first paratroop regiment," she whispered softly, and then left the room. Rolf, a Czech in the next bed chimed in. "I guess you pulled what you Americans call a Boner, eh?"

"Alright, don't rub it in. How was I to know?"

"You should have asked me. Where do you think I got this bad leg? It was okay until a week ago, and then it acted up again and here I am."

"What was it like?"

"It was two thousand Legionnaires being slaughtered by forty thousand communist troops. It was a 56-day siege at an outpost called Isabellel. They stood them off in the last eight hours and died in a final charge with bayonets bared. Babette's young Niles was one of the victims. Weeks before I had received a lucky wound and was carried to safety by helicopter. Later on, the only way into Dien Bien Phu was by parachute. There was no way out."

"I'm glad I missed that one," I said.

"It was rough going. We were called the fighting fools of Dien Bien Phu. The odds against us were too much. Not only were there thousands of Reds, but heavy rains made air supply almost impossible. Food ran low, ammunition was going, and the crazy Reds kept coming in."

"You're a lucky man," I said.

"Yes, I thank God for that. I was in Hanoi when the end came. General Christian De Castries sent a last message to Hanoi. I recall it now as it was told to me. 'I am calling from the middle of the fighting. The Communists are everywhere. The situation is very grave. Combat is confused and goes on all about. I feel the end is approaching, but we will fight to the finish.' A half hour later another voice, unidentified, was picked up saying, 'In five minutes, everything will be gone here. The Communists are only yards away. A salute to all.' There was a crackle of static and then silence. Dien Bien Phu had fallen."

"How did you get over to the Legion in the first place, Rolf?"

"The communists took over my country and work was hard to come by. I had a mistress and she told me she was pregnant. It was really difficult for me to leave her, but I could not support both of us, along with a child. All we had to eat was bread and potatoes. When I crossed the border I was picked up, and they sent me to a refugee camp in Trieste."

"How did you get over to France to enlist?"

"That was easy. I knew if I told them I was starving back home they would have me sent there anyway. So I told them I was escaping religious persecution and they sent me to France and I was put to work in a coal mine. But that back-breaking work was not for me. So I hopped the border to Germany, where I was arrested once again and shipped back to France. It was then that I decided on a try at life in la Légion. Life was miserable in Czechoslovakia, but compared to the legion, it now doesn't look so bad."

As I began dropping off to sleep I recalled the many misleading novels, movies and television stories of the glamorous and exciting Legion. If only someone would paint a true picture of the sordid story of hard work, brutality, and ugly death. If I ever made it to the outside world, I felt I could tell the true story of the Legion of lost and damned souls.

CHAPTER 16

As the days passed I slowly regained my strength. It wouldn't be long before I would be rejoining my outfit. Down at the end of the ward was a battle-scarred veteran by the name of Lucian. He had really been worked over by the NLF when captured while scouting ahead of our troops in the mountains. Only the rapid arrival of his comrades saved Lucian from being emasculated. However, he was savagely beaten, and now it seems as though he was losing his last battle. The ward was silent as Lucian began singing one of his favorite Legion songs entitled *"En Algeria."*

"En Algerie, sur une colline" -- In Algeria, on a hill.

"Un Legionnaire, monte la garde" -- A Legionnaire stands

Fran Lucca

guard. *"Auprès de son comrade touche à mort par une balle
rebelle"--* After his comrade struck dead by a rebel bullet.
"Camarade, et vous mon pays" -- Comrade, and you my
country. *"Je vous laisse sans regret"* -- I leave you without
regret. *"Volontairement, je servais bien"* -- Voluntarily, I
served well. *"Avec honneur et fidélité"* -- With honor and
fidelity. *"Un Légionnaire quand il tombe"* -- A Legionnaire
when he falls. *"Quand il ferme les yeux"* -- When he closes
his eyes. *"Il repose en Algérie"* -- He rests in Algeria. *"Sur
la colline, une croix à raconter."* -- On the hill, one cross
to tell.

A few moments later, Lucien was dead. As he was
wheeled out I made the Sign of the Cross. I was feeling
very sad and wasn't in the mood for reading, so I decided
to send the folks a letter.

Laghouat, Algerie. Oct. 5, 1957

Dear Mom and Dad,

I received your letter of September
23 yesterday. As usual word from
you made me feel real fine. I will
tell you of my present sickness and
hospitalization, Mom and Dad, only
because it happens to bring me the
most comfort in spiritual peace since
my engagement in the Legion. I have
jaundice. My skin and eyes were quite

150

yellow. At present though, I seem to be regaining a whiter appearance. Except for the first four or five days before I came to the hospital and was very sick and doing my work at the same time, the disease has given comparative joy to my existence here. I feel quite weak, but it doesn't matter because I have only to read or lie in my bed when I am sleepy. This luck has given me my first real chance since I've been in the Legion to calmly read a book and find a tranquil spirit. For the first time in quite a while, this morning I studied French. By reading magazines I can grasp the general meaning of just about everything in French writing. I can understand practically all I hear when listening to French being spoken by a Frenchman who speaks in a slow and even way, such as a Parisian. The others, such as the Germans or Italians, I understand very well.

My engagement in the Legion was a slap in the face of mother experience, insofar as what I learned while a crewman on the Appian. My other traveling also brought to me a knowledge of the road. I saw the lovely creations and variations of nature. The traveling road unfolded changing characteristics in people. Then the bloody leg, on which is too much of a tale. The height and depth of all experiences and emotions other than that of Job. All of this to form my new perception in the reading of literature. I'll be darned if the perception is worth the price.

My prayers are for your life's contentment.

Your son,
Ronnie

CHAPTER 17

It was with a sinking heart that I surveyed the remote possibility of escape. To flee from the heart of the desert would be suicide. Not only would I have the Legion and French Army looking for me, but the Arabs would turn me in for the bounty. Or maybe I would end up castrated and then tortured to death by the fellagha. There would be little opportunity for living off the land if I made good my escape from the hospital. No matter in which direction I ran I would be facing serious hazards. If I went further south, I would only be going into more French territory and more desert, stretching for hundreds of miles. If I went west, I faced the almost impossible task of crossing desert and mountains to reach

Morocco. If I did reach Morocco I probably would be killed by the natives there. Unfriendly desert and hostile Arabs faced me also if I took off east toward Tunisia or Libya. The last direction left was north, and if I went that way I would be entering the area in which most of the French regular army and civilians were located. I was filled with despair, caused also by the failure of my parents' efforts to secure my release. My previous failure in escaping and the resulting jolt in the Legion prison was prominent in my mind. The future not only looked bleak, but practically hopeless. Was there any way to escape?

"Why so serious, soldier? Life in la Légion can't be that bad." said the French doctor as he stepped over to my bed. It was Captain Le Gare, a veteran of many years' service with the French regular army.

"It is nothing, captain," I answered. "Just a bit of homesickness, I guess."

"Eh, you will get used to the life of a soldier. Sometimes the service does strange things to a man's outlook."

"Do you have a family, captain?" I asked.

"I have a wife and three sons, one of whom is now attending St. Cyr. I had a brother who also was a soldier." His face strained at the thought.

"What happened to him, captain?" I asked.

"It all began in 1940," he went on to explain. "We had been in WWII for a year. I was pushed in with a patrol which helped hold off the Germans at Dunkirk. I managed to escape and continued with the free French under General De Gaulle. However, my brother joined up with the Vichy forces. I learned later that he was killed near Oran in 1942. I was serving near there at the time."

"I'm sorry, captain. I can see I was just feeling sorry for myself." However, the doctor's next words stirred within me a feeling of new hope.

"Incidentally. private." he stated, "you'll be leaving here shortly for a thirty-day convalescence at the Legion rest camp at Arzew. That's on the Mediterranean near Oran."

"My God," I yelled. "I still have a chance--" and then I cut myself short. I had nearly given away my constant anxiety about escaping.

"A chance for what, Legionnaire?"

"A chance for a little fun and frolic before I go back to my company, captain. I am most grateful."

Captain Le Gare smiled, turned to walk out of the ward and said, "Bon voyage. Reynolds."

I wonder how he meant that. Did he surmise and secretly hope for my freedom? I said goodbye to my fellow patients and took just essential gear and a rifle to protect myself, if ambushed by the NLF. The rest of my stuff was left at the fort, but I hoped that I would never need any of it again. I made still another vow not to return.

I took a truck to Jelfa and went the rest of the way by train. The rehabilitation camp at Arzew was quite a contrast from the desert fort. Some Legionnaires got a furlough here after forty-two months' service. Others came for a rest after a wound or illness. Rest camp or not, we still pulled guard duty and work details. The captain in charge was a real madman. He had few men under him for the work detail and would make excuses to arrest the new men when the occasion would arise. Minor infractions such as dust in your area during inspection usually got you a couple of days' restriction, which was a chance for the captain to get you on his corveés. On one of the few days when I wasn't doing the captain's dirty work I went to the canteen for some beer. A friendly shout came from the end of the smoke-filled room.

"Hey, Yankee Doodle Ron, how did you fake it in here?"

"Well, I'll be damned," I exclaimed. "Chicolomano Di Blazi. The last time I saw you was at Ghardaia. How did you nose your way into here?"

"Sit down, Garcon," I said. He grinned at me. "While we are waiting for our wine, Chicki, tell me what has happened to you?"

"Shortly after you left Ghardaia I was in the front end of a truck convoy making our way back to the fort when the fellagha salauds ambushed us. I got it clean through the arm. I was lucky though. You remember

Lazio, the young Belgian who always carried the picture of the beautiful brunette nude he was going to marry one day? Well, a bullet hit him in the head, killed him instantly. Look Ron, here is her picture."

"Damn, that's a shame. Lazio was a good man. Let me see that picture. The poor devil. He sure is missing a lot. *Mon Dieu!* She's all femme. But why did you keep this picture?"

"Ron, what would you have me do? I figured the picture would preserve her lovely image. Would you want this picture to be sent home to his mother? Besides, copain, I've had a friendly exchange of letters with this gorgeous mademoiselle. Her name is Cristol."

"All of you Neapolitans are the same," I laughed. "Let's have another vino."

"Now, Ron, tell me about yourself. Are you still thinking of escape after what the mad Turk did to you when you were captured?"

"Don't remind me of that madman, Chicki. Let's not think of the past, but instead let us toast the future when we hope to be free again."

"I drink to that, Ron. I will even help it to come true."

"What do you mean? Are you going to swim across the Mediterranean to sunny Italy?" I quipped.

"That's exactly what we shall do Johnny."

"Di Blazi, you've had enough vino for one night. Only a nut would try a stunt like that."

157

"All the more reason it might be. successful because the Legion would not dream anyone would be so stupid as to try it. What do you say, shall we give it a try?"

"It's a wild plan. Let's hear the details."

"It is simple. We will meet here tomorrow after duty and then walk into town on pass. Then we make our way to the waterfront, get rid of our clothes, and swim out into the sea until we find an Arab in a small boat. We will then force him to take us to freedom."

"I'm game, but it's a one-in-a-million chance," I said. "It is still better than sweating out more years in this outfit. I will meet you here at 4:30 tomorrow afternoon, and I hope your swimming muscles are in good shape."

"Sleep well, and say an extra prayer tonight. Until tomorrow."

CHAPTER 18

That night I had a tough time getting to sleep. I kept
waking up with nightmares of being swallowed up by
the blue-green waters of the sea. When dawn finally
came I didn't feel any more rested than when I first
hit the sack. My minor chores that day seemed to drag
on forever. My mind continually reverted to Chicki
and escape. In one way, I figured I had nothing to lose
and everything to gain. I got off a bit early and went
to the canteen. Chicki was on clean-up detail there
and wouldn't be free for another hour. I was getting
edgy, and told him I would meet him in a well known
bistro near the waterfront. He smiled and nodded
in agreement. I didn't drink too much for fear that

it would interfere with the task ahead. This seemed like a good time to write a note home, just in case something went wrong. I got some writing materials from the bistro proprietor.

Oct. 3rd, 1957, Arzew.

Dear Mom and Dad,

Received your letter of Oct. 10th just before leaving the desert to come here by the sea. It seems like everyone has adapted to this Legion life but me. The Legion is such a distressing symbol of man's corruptness and failure. It seems an impossible dream that I am here, and likewise when it's actually all over, it will be hard to believe that it ever happened. Ah, but this writing must sound exactly as that which I wrote one year ago. But then, the most puzzling, incomprehensible thing of all, is that I realize that I needed the Legion to teach me those sacred things I didn't understand, yet the time of the lesson has all but burst me, and the continuance gives me ominous biddings.

My intent in writing this letter was to send my love and my everlasting

160

wishes for your happiness. Also, to let you know that I may not be able to write for awhile, and if I don't, please do not worry. I'm not sure of this, but just in case, I don't want you to worry. Goodbye for the present, Mom and Dad.

Your loving son,
Ronnie

It was a mile hike into town from the camp on top of the hill, and Chicki seemed a bit bushed from the trek. Arzew was half-European, and half-Arab. A Legionnaire always took a little risk going into town because of the NLF elements. Rumor had it that many a Legionnaire had disappeared in Arzew, especially those that entered the off-limits Casbah section.

"Are you all set, Ron?" asked Chicki.

"As ready as ever," I grunted. "Here, have a shot of cognac before we leave."

The proprietor, Jean, had become friendly during my short stay at Arzew. He and his lovely wife Marie made me feel like one of the family. Later they would come in very handy to me. Jean and Marie were not their real names. To reveal their names would surely jeopardize their lives. Marie came over with two cognacs.

"Hello Ron, who is your friend?"

"This is Chicki, Marie. Chicolomano Di Blazi to be more proper. He's an ancien copain from one of my earlier assignments."

"Hello Chicki Di Blazi, are you looking for some of our girls?"

"Oh no, Marie, not today. We have other plans for this evening."

"That's right, Marie, we'll take a raincheck," I added.

"Oui," she purred, as she walked away.

"Come on Ron, let's get started," ordered the impatient Chicki.

"Right. So long Jean, Marie," I shouted. "Au revoir!" they answered.

Dusk had arrived and there was a chill in the breeze as we made our way to the waterfront. This was hazardous because we had to skirt the Casbah, and the swish of a blade could come at any time. Within moments we could smell the salt air, mixed with the stink of dead fish and seaweed.

"Well Chicki, here we are. Strip to your underclothes and tie your shoes and shirt in your pants. We'll strap them to our backs and swim out."

"Si, Ron, let's hope we find an Arab boat soon." We stepped into the water together.

"It's cold!" cried Chicki.

"Jeez, colder than a witch's tits," I chattered.

"Start swimming and you'll warm up," encouraged Chicki. We got about a quarter of a mile from shore and still saw no sign of any boat.

"Ron, my gonads are frosted and tired enough to drop off. Should we go back?

"Hang on. Switch your clothes to your chest and float on your back awhile. We'll make it."

I was becoming exhausted myself. It had been more than a year since I had done any swimming. I was out of shape. A low hum broke the silence of the evening and both of us froze on the spot. The sound of the motor became louder.

"It's a French patrol boat," I whispered. "Quiet, and tread water."

Chicki exclaimed excitedly, "It's headed this way. Look, there's the spotlight. God, we're right on her course!"

"Don't panic," I implored. "Follow me." We swam quietly about a hundred yards and stopped. The drone of the engine got louder, and we could make out the sharp prow less than five hundred yards away in the moonlit calm of the Mediterranean. The sleek craft roared toward us, it's spotlight knifing the night in a sweeping motion. When it was about one hundred yards away Chicki gave the signal.

"Dive, and count up to fifty slowly before coming up."

It seemed like an eternity down there and I speeded up the count after forty. My lungs were bursting and the pressure in my ears became unbearable. I had to surface. When I did, the fantail of the patrol boat was visible off in the distance, and getting smaller and smaller as it zoomed out of sight. With a sigh of relief, I swam about looking for Chicki. He bobbed up nearby and called out.

"We made it, amigo. *Madre Mia,* but that was close."

"Chicki, I'm not up to anymore close calls like that one. I hate to admit it, but it looks hopeless. If we don't find an Arab boat soon, we're done for."

"Ron, I'm sorry, but my arm with the wound, she has gone numb. I cannot lift it. I cannot go on. Go back to shore and don't worry about me. I will take my time. I'll make it back."

"Leave you hell! We're in this together. Come on, we'll swim together. Rest your arm on my hip. We'll make it back together." It took almost two hours to swim the torturous quarter-mile back to the beach. When we hit the white sand, both of us fell forward, exhausted and sick to our stomachs, but alive. We put on our wet clothing and made it back inside the post with only seconds to spare before the gates were locked. Our clothes had partially dried during the hike back. Another attempt to free myself from the Legion had failed. It was another escape to nowhere.

CHAPTER 19

Time was running out for me, as I had only a few days left at Arzew. I had to get away before being shipped back to the Sahara. Chicki had already given up and had volunteered to go back to his desert fighting outfit. I got another pass and headed for Jean and Marie's bistro in hopes of formulating another escape plan over a couple of drinks.

"Hello Ron," welcomed Jean. "Why so serious tonight?"

"My days are numbered," I said. Marie came up close to me carrying a tray of empty glasses. The strong French perfume accentuated her loveliness as she cooed, *"Mon cher,* we cannot bear to see you so. *Que pouvons-nous faire pour vous?"*

Jean interrupted with a chuckle. "Don't look so puzzled. What my wife is suggesting, is offering you the services of one of our girls. There are many rooms upstairs."

"No... No. That is not what I want now. I'm getting desperate. There is so little time left."

"Listen, Ron," said Jean. "See those two sailors sitting at the last table against the wall? One is British and the other is Canadian. I overheard them expressing a desire to jump ship and join la Légion étrangère. "You take it from there, ami."

I lost little time. I tossed some francs on the bar, grabbed a bottle of wine, and made my way to their table.

"Mind if an ally joins the party, mates?" I asked.

"Well, if it doesn't sound like a Yank," exclaimed the Limey as he gazed at my Legion uniform.

"Welcome aboard," chimed in the Canadian sailor. "What's a Yank doing in that outfit?" asked the Englishman.

"It's a long story, friend, but I'd give an arm if I could be back in civvies in good old Buffalo, New York, USA." I answered.

"Say, that's near Niagara Falls," said the Canadian. I live in Quebec," he added.

"Only a stone's throw," I answered. "Where do you hail from?" I asked the Englishman.

"I come from the dock area of Liverpool," he replied. "My name is Sheldon, and my buddy here is named Hill," he said.

"Glad to know you fellas. My name is Ron."

"Our ships are berthed in the harbor. We're in the Merchant Marine, and it's damned dull," said Sheldon.

"You boys are lucky, I said as I gave them a generous portion of my wine. "I only wish to hell I was pulling out with you."

"Well, that's a coincidence," said Hill. "We were just remarking that it would be exciting to jump ship and join your outfit. That German sergeant over there told us what a slam-bang fighting bunch you fellows were. He all but signed us up."

I glanced over at the table Hill indicated, and terror swept through me. I met the piercing stare of Sergeant Gunther. He was a sadistic ex-Gestapo man. I looked away and whispered, "Look men, maybe we can arrange a deal, but not here in the open. That sergeant would slit my throat in a second if he knew what I was trying to do. Tell you what, Sheldon, you follow me into the john--the head--and we'll make some plans." Sheldon and Hill followed me into the latrine.

"Listen men," I cautioned. "Let me level with you. First of all, let me tell you that you would be making a fatal mistake in signing up with the Legion. You'll be nothing but slaves for five years. It's a rotten world of fighting, building roads, marching, meager pay and food, and sadistic officers. Within days you would be trying to escape. It's highly unromantic and often fatal. The only reason the sergeant fed you that tale is because there is a bonus paid to all officers and noncoms for any sucker they recruit."

"Right!" said Sheldon. "You've talked us out of it, but we still want to jump ship. I'll give you my papers and you can go aboard my ship in my place tomorrow night. By the time they find out who you really are, you'll be a long way from Algeria. In return, give me a little money and I'll take a train to Oran. What do you say?"

"It's a deal, Sheldon." I took his identification card and secreted it inside my grouch bag. The old athletic-supporter-turned-secret-purse was still holding up. I went back to the fort that night almost hysterical with anxiety. In another day I might be a free man again.

The next day I was just about finished with my corveé, and was making plans for a pass, when Sergeant Gunther came up to me with a glare in his eyes and a smirk on his face.

"Alright, Reynolds," he snapped. "The captain wants to see you. *Macht schnell!* On the double!" My blood turned to ice water with the dread feeling that my escape plan had been discovered. I trembled under Gunther's touch. The captain was a rugged looking Frenchman, squat in appearance, with a scar extending from under his left eye to the tip of his chin. His grayish-green eyes were penetrating and menacing.

"I presume you know why I have sent for you, private?" he asked curtly.

"Non, mon capitain," I replied, desperately trying to look innocent.

"Were you not in a bistro last night in the Rue de Ie Mer?"

"Yes I was, Captain, but I did not get into any trouble."

"Well, then, soldier, let me ask you this. Did you meet two sailors?" I could feel my heart pounding, and I became slightly nauseous at the thought that my plot had been uncovered. My voice was a bit unsteady when I answered.

"Yes, Captain, I did make the acquaintance of two sailors. We had a few glasses of wine together. But there was no trouble."

"It has been brought to my attention," the Captain growled, "that you discouraged the sailors from joining our Legion by making derogatory remarks about our outfit. I have reported the sailors to their captain. Your punishment is four days' confinement to the post. You can spend the time on corveés and trying to think better of la Légion." A feeling of relief swept over me as I realized that my escape plan had not been revealed by the sailors. As I was led away, it dawned on me that the next four days were all that I had left at Arzew before being sent back to the desert. No wonder the captain had been so easy on me. On the other hand, how could

I ever make a break for it now? I was temporarily panic-stricken. My first impulse was to take off immediately and keep running until shot down. Fortunately, I managed to shy away from this wild idea. Perhaps I could come up with another escape plan during my four days of confinement. God must have been with me, for somehow I managed to muster enough strength to keep up my courage and spirit. There still might be a chance to get away.

As I went about my details, I thought of my relatives praying for me. We always had been a religious family. I could picture Mom and Dad making novenas for me, and Grandma and Grandpa lighting candles at church for my safe return. Mom mentioned that a vigil light burned before the statue of the Blessed Virgin Mary in our hallway since the day I left. How I longed to be able to drop to my knees before the "Lovely Lady Dressed In Blue."

A letter from home came telling me that everything possible was being done to have me released from the Legion. President Eisenhower had acknowledged a letter from my folks, and passed it on to the State Department. This department was still trying to get me out, on the grounds that I was underage when I enlisted. My father had been in touch with Walter Kanitz, author of "White Kepi" in his Canadian home less than two hundred miles from Buffalo. He was not optimistic. He urged my parents not to do anything foolish, and warned that a desertion attempt could lead to my death. Mr. Kanitz didn't pull any punches. He said that there was very little that could be done to get a Legionnaire discharged before the end of his five-year hitch.

My parents were quite impressed with our Congressman, Edmond P. Radwan, a Republican from the 41st congressional district of New York State. He turned his office over to them whenever they went to Washington to plead my case. Our Congressman saw to it that Mom and Dad were interviewed by the highest officials possible in the State Department who would be concerned with a case of this type. Mr. Radwan pointed out that it had taken months before the State Department had finally made formal representations to the French government in Paris. This had not been done until Congressman Radwan had called the case to the attention of Assistant Secretary of State Robert C. Hill. The Congressman further revealed that nothing had been accomplished by the lengthy negotiations with French authorities in Algiers. Mr. Radwan even got the runaround from the French Ambassador, Hervé Alphand. All the Congressman got was the Ambassador's sympathetic interest.

The Buffalo Evening News Washington Bureau also published stories, which helped spur on the State Department to greater efforts. Consul General Lewis Clark tried his best, but his efforts were futile. Under different circumstances, all this high level activity would be quite flattering. However, we were not succeeding and I was becoming more and more discouraged. There seemed to be no doubt about it--the French were deliberately stalling. Outside efforts to obtain my release were getting nowhere. I didn't feel that I could stand it much longer. There was only a faint hope for future success. Time was running out, and I was becoming desperate. Well, I'd put an end to all of this pussy-footing one way or another, come tomorrow. Only hours were left. Tomorrow morning might be my last chance to escape. They would be marching me to the depot for my trip back into the desert. It was my great hope that this was one train ride that I would not take.

CHAPTER 20

The day dawned gloomy and overcast, but my spirits were high. A corporal-chef came to my cell and barked, "You, Reynolds, get your gear. You are being shipped back to Ghardaia within the hour." It didn't take me long to pack my belongings. I took only my essential personal property and stuffed the rest in a closet. I figured I'd have to travel light when I made a break for it.

We marched outdoors to waiting trucks, which carried us the short distance to Oran. In the city we lined up near the railroad depot for our trip deep into the Sahara. My head was dizzy with wild thoughts of freedom. I waited until I had reached the depot door when I suddenly stepped aside and told the corporal

I wished to check my gear on the platform. So far, so good. I walked slowly toward the stacked knapsacks and ditty bags, and pretended to read the name tags. Everyone, including the corporal, was inside the depot waiting to board the old train. I stepped hastily into the shadows with my bag, and made my way to the rear of the depot. Then I walked briskly away from the station to a nearby street and hailed a taxicab. It seemed too simple.

The cabby eyed me suspiciously until I told him I was on leave for forty-eight hours and was in search of a good but inexpensive hotel. A few francs brought out a smile and a quick response.

"Oui, monsieur, aussitot."

Within ten minutes we stopped before a third-rate hotel on a dingy side street, but it would do. I told the cab driver to wait for me while I registered and brought my small ditty bag with personal effects. The clerk was a thin, greasy little character with pince-nez glasses and a thin pencil-line mustache. He eyed me cautiously until I threw ten francs on the counter and asked, *"Avez-vous un lit?"* He answered that he had a one bedroom and escorted me to the second floor. After he left I went to the end of the hall and placed a telephone call to Arzew at Jean and Marie's place.

"Hello Ronnie," said Jean, "Where are you calling from?"

"Quiet, and don't use my name. I'm in Oran, and haven't much time. I need your help, and quick."

"You name it, and it is yours."

"I'll need a change of clothes, something in the civilian line. I'll be down to pick it up soon."

"It'll be waiting for you. When you get here, go right upstairs, and Marie will see to it that you are taken care of."

I went back to my room, locked the door, and headed back down the stairs two at a time. The driver was waiting as promised, and it was off to Arzew again. I had to be very careful that none of the Legion noncoms spotted me. It was early for them to be in the bistro, but still, I had to be careful. It seemed like an eternity over the dusty, winding road. When we pulled up in front of Jean and Marie's, I threw a bunch of franc notes at the cabby, and told him to come back in one hour for the trip back to Oran.

The place was practically empty. Fortunately, there were no Legionnaires out on pass yet. Jean greeted me with a big smile, and nodded toward the stairway. Then he reached under the bar and pushed a buzzer. As I neared the top of the stairs a door on the right of the landing opened, and there stood Marie. She was indeed a most beautiful woman, with long shiny black hair down to her bare shoulders. Her off-the-shoulder blouse showed signs of bursting under the strain of her ample bosom.

"Follow me, *cher. Vite.*"

She led me down the long hallway to the last room. I had seen dozens of patrons climb these stairs, cheek to cheek with the sensuous Marie, or with either of the two French waitresses. However, for some reason, I was never solicited. Maybe it was because of the warm feeling of friendship among the three of us. She ushered me into the room and locked the door behind her. She pulled a package from under a cot and dumped out its contents.

"Here, quickly, take off your uniform and put on these."

"But, Marie, I can't until you leave."

"You foolish boy!" she laughed. "I have had hundreds of fine specimens such as you here in this room. I will not blush."

I stepped into. a pair of black slacks and slipped on a black turtle necked sweater. Next I put on a pair of sandals, and topped my disguise with a beret and a pair of sunglasses. I wrapped my uniform and kepi in a newspaper to be disposed of later. I walked to the door. Marie looked up into my eyes and placed her arms around my neck.

"Good luck and bon voyage, *mon cher,*" she whispered as our lips touched. I held her close for a moment, then put her at arm's length and went out the door and down the stairway. I stopped at the bar on my way out to thank Jean.

He jested, "What will you have stranger?" I laughed nervously. *"Sacre bleu,* even your own mother would have to look twice before recognizing you." Jean poured two glasses of cognac and toasted to the future. After a handshake I picked up my package and hurried out the door.

I found the cabby, and had a tough time convincing him in my best French that the Legionnaire who had hired him had been ordered back to the fort on an emergency call. I offered to take the ride back to Oran. He hesitated at first, but a fistful of francs changed his mind. Money saved up in the hospital was coming in handy, and I was spending as if it were my last day on this earth.

Once back at the hotel I lingered outside until the desk clerk was out of sight. Then I slipped in and made it to my room unnoticed. I tucked the newspaper with my uniform into a dresser drawer, and then slipped back out of my room. From the top of the stairs I observed the clerk. When he was called to one of the ground floor rooms, I quietly descended and made my way out to the street. It was still light out, and I took a taxi to the waterfront.

The sight of the beautiful Mediterranean was marred by the cluster of French ships. Then my eyes fixed on a different, but most welcome sight--a dirty little boat flying the British ensign--the steamer Usmouth. I approached the ship and spotted a deck hand suspended halfway down the starboard side on a scaffold painting the bow.

"Hi there matey, where do you hail from?" I asked. The surprised sailor nearly fell from his perch.

"Well, I'll be," he exclaimed. "You talk like a Yank."

"I am. The name is Ron Reynolds."

"Glad to know you, Reynolds. My name is Rick. I'm from Manchester, England. Where are you from?"

"A place called Buffalo, in New York State, not too far from Niagara Falls."

"Oh yes, I've heard of those cities. What are you doing in this bloody hell hole, and in those clothes?" I spent the next half hour telling Rick of my plight. He listened intently, then said, "I've got an idea. You be here at eight PM and make your way aboard. Better yet, meet me at the African Bar at that time. I'll bring some friends along, and we'll work out some plans." My terror was being relieved to some extent.

"It's a deal, my friend. You'll be saving my life."

As I made my way back from the waterfront, I caught a last glimpse of what I hoped was my passport to freedom--the black and white, dirty little tramp steamer, which held more promise to me than a luxurious ocean liner.

CHAPTER 21

That evening I hurried to the African Bar with high hopes. It had seemed too good to be true. Then my hopes became shattered. No one there looked even remotely like a British sailor, and none showed up all night. Finally, bitterly disappointed, I went down to the dock and approached the Usmouth. Not a soul was around except an Arab guard on the gangplank. This Arab was highly suspicious and appeared hostile. It seemed better not to push things too far, so I lingered nearby for hours, but with no results. Eventually I returned to my hotel room.

The next morning, I knew that I had to do something. Hotels were required by law to report all visitors to the police. Much of this was routine red tape, and it might be possible to escape discovery for a day or two, but sooner or later it would be inevitable. Occasionally, Legionnaires of several years' experience would check into hotels and get into civilian clothes in order to date the local French girls. Most of the damsels would not associate with a Legionnaire in uniform. My strategy was to make the clerk think that I was one of these Legionnaires. I went out and purchased a large bouquet of cheap flowers. The clerk did a double-take when I entered. He stopped me as I started for the stairway.

"What's the matter, mon ami" I said cheerfully. "Can't a Legionnaire get out of uniform without causing a riot? You know the femme wouldn't be seen dead with a Legionnaire. Now you wouldn't want to stand in the way of a little romance, would you?" The desk clerk giggled. He was still chuckling when I climbed the stairs to my room. I lay on my bed figuring out my next move. I would walk out of the hotel with the flowers, pretending to have a date. Then I would ditch the bouquet. That should throw any pursuers off my track.

I grabbed the bouquet of flowers and started down the stairs. I gave the desk clerk a sly wink, and he uttered an obscenity and giggled as I left the hotel. I walked for several blocks, circling back once or twice, in case I was being followed. I wasn't. Finally I came to a cinema. This seened like a good place in which to hide and think. I don't even remember what was showing on the screen.

My thoughts continued to return to the plan to go to the waterfront and try to get on that British ship. After an hour I worked up nerve to leave the movie, and walked back to the dock area. I knew that there was an Arab guard at the gangplank of the Usmouth. They pulled guard duty on all foreign ships at dock. My plan was to pretend to be an English sailor coming back from shore leave. If I could get by the Arab, I would then have to confront the British Officer of the Deck. I could speak French to the O.D. and try to convince him that I was a colonist friend wishing to visit with Rick. Once I saw Rick something could be worked out. I couldn't think of anything else to do.

I reached the ship. No sailors were around, and there was no sign of Rick. I took a deep breath, uttered a short prayer under my breath, and boldly walked up the gangplank. Facing me was the fierce looking Arab guard, armed with a rifle. I kept right on walking, and smiled at the guard. I said in English, in what I hoped was a British accent, "I've had enough of this town for the day." The guard stared at me, grunted, then nodded his head.

Fortunately, I was familiar with ships and the customs of the officers and men from my time in the Norwegian Merchant Marine. I could walk around most merchant ships with some degree of familiarity. So far, so good. As I turned on to the quarter deck I met a lieutenant. He must be the O.D.

"Auriez-vous la bonte de m'indiquer le chemin aller a Seaman Rick?" I asked in my best French, which was about the only good thing I had picked up in the Legion. The Officer of the Deck seemed puzzled, but managed to catch Rick's name.

"Is it Rick you would be wanting to see?" he asked.

"Oui monsieur." He pointed to the after-deck, and I made my way to the stern. Rick was seated on the fantail with two other sailors, and he jumped up when I approached. "Well I'll be damned!" he yelled. Then he said, "We couldn't get off last night." When the officer was out of earshot, he said, "We'll stow you away somehow."

He introduced me to the seamen. The three of them shuffled me down a ladder to a large hold filled to near capacity with bales of Alfa grass.

"Here is where your home will be for the next few days," I was told. "We'll make a tunnel."

They managed to dig me a two-by-six-foot hole. I wasted little time in crawling into it. It wasn't the most comfortable spot in the world, but by far the most welcome one in eighteen months. My friends managed to smuggle me food and water. However, I was not able to leave my concealment for over a week. It began to seem like an eternity. I would have felt better if we were on the high seas, instead of at the dock within the reach of the French. The tunnel soon became quite uncomfortable. Sometimes the blood stopped circulating in my legs. At times I felt that anything would be better than lying in this grave. Then I would reflect on life in the Legion, and managed to endure. The air was foul with dirt, sweat, and the necessities of nature. Unfortunately, the ship was held at the dock for eleven extra days. It was waiting for more cargo, which was delayed by Arabs who were attacking the trains bringing the Alfa grass from the interior. Several other ordinary seamen were let in on the secret. Some of them seemed to think they were taking part in some kind of a game, and acted as though the whole episode was some sort of a lark. To me it meant life and death. Finally, one of them took care of the serious problem, which might have led to my exposure. This fellow was known as Krieger. He was a short, balding, serious sailor, who had fled from Germany to get away from Hitler. He sized up the situation quickly and managed to impress upon the others that extreme caution was necessary. He organized a timetable for the delivery of food and water, and got the others to stay clear of me at the times they were not on the job aiding me.

On the eleventh day Rick came over to the tunnel. He whispered, "Have a little more patience, if you can. The cargo has arrived, and we should be upping anchor in a few hours."

"Thank God!" I exclaimed. At that moment, a loud commotion sent me into near panic. I could make out excited French jargon.

"Stay put, I'll be back later," cautioned Rick. He hustled topside, and I crouched in my tunnel, dreading the worst. The rapid French chatter came closer, mixed with remarks uttered in English. Then I heard a voice, presumably that of the captain.

"But Lieutenant Bouchard, it is highly improbable that one of your Legionnaires is stowed away on my ship. We have kept a sharp watch these two weeks in port."

"Ce n'est pas ma faute. Captain, I have a job to do. We have reason to believe that a Finn named Finch was last seen along the dock near the bales of Alfa grass which have been consigned to your ship. It is my duty to search every inch of this boat."

"Very well, lieutenant," the captain said. "You may poke around these bales all you want, but we get underway in a few hours." Footsteps came nearer, and I could hear the searcher jabbing his bayonet into the bales of grass. I trembled with fear when the steps halted less than two feet from my hideout. Peering through the grass cargo I could see his combat boots. My heart pounded so loud that I was afraid the thumping could be heard outside of the tunnel. Then I heard a rustling noise, and a blade came sliding through, about two inches from my nose.

I stared at the shiny steel and was ready to make a break for it, futile as it might be. The soldier yelled, "One more plunge here and then on to the next bale." I steadied myself for the expected disaster. I shut my eyes and held my breath. I was praying. But the blade never came. The yelling of men on deck could be heard. There were screams in French and English. *"Arrêtez!* You there, halt! *Qu'y a-t-il?* After him, he's getting away." Then came three rifle shots and more hollering and confusion. The sound of the chase began to fade, and I surmised that the Finn had made it off the boat. I heard two more shots and shouting in the distance, and then it was quiet. My whole body was saturated with perspiration. My mouth was dry. My chest was burning. And my heart kept up its pounding. I began to panic all over again when I heard footsteps nearby. But I calmed down when I recognized Rick's voice.

"It's alright. They're gone. The Legionnaire is running along the waterfront, and the others are after him. They are all off this ship. A bale of Alfa was being loaded on the deck when it hit another bale and knocked it over, exposing the hidden deserter. I think the worst is over now. It shouldn't be too long before we get underway. Stay put."

"OK, Rick," I whispered back. "Believe me, nothing will get me out of here until we set sail. I lay back, which didn't require much movement, and sighed in relief. Then I prayed, thanking God for protecting me. For the first time I began to think that my escape would be successful. I nearly cried.

Later, my solitude was interrupted by a familiar rumbling. The engines had kicked over, Oh, what a sweet sound! Then I felt myself lurched to one side.

Moments later I heard the waves splashing against the sides of the ship. I wanted to crash out of tunnel and cheer at the top of my lungs. But I knew better. It wouldn't take much to put back into port and turn me over to the French authorities. I had to play it cool now, with success so close. I knew that I had to be careful for the remainder of the voyage, however long it took. When we were underway a few hours Rick and his friends came down to my hiding place. We all shook hands. The boys even broke out a small container of rum, and we toasted a victory.

"I'll never be able to repay you, but I'll never forget what you've done," I told them. "You saved my life. My undying thanks to all of you."

"Forget it," said Rick with a big smile. "We were glad to give a mate in trouble a helping hand."

CHAPTER 22

The next several days were uneventful as we headed for the British Isles. Most of my time was spent sleeping, either in my tunnel, or underneath the bunk of one of my benefactors. During the daily inspection, the sailors would smuggle me from cabin to cabin, or back to my tunnel. No one else knew I was aboard.

In my waking moments I thought of the wonderful, unbelievable freedom which I was now regaining. I thought of Mom and Dad and Sis back home. I also thought about going to Mass and Communion, a privilege I had not been allowed for a year and a half. Visions of a few beers in Ontario across the Niagara River with the boys would come to me, as well as taking in a dance with some cute blonde. I visualized scenes of playing hockey under the bridge near the Art Gallery, or a game of baseball at Delaware Park. God has been good to me, and I had a lot to do to make it up to Him.

The North Atlantic was a bit rough, but I didn't get seasick. My service on the Appian had conditioned me to the rolling and tossing. I was in Rick's cabin the final day of my cruise to freedom when suddenly the waves disappeared and the ship tossed no more. The sun shone brightly as the ship settled down to a glide. Looking out of the porthole I could see hills of rolling green.

"Are we here Rick? One minute we are being plagued by thunderous waves, and now it is calm and peaceful. What is this?"

"We have just entered the Firth of Clyde. That is Scotland you see. We will be pulling into port in a few minutes at Grenoch. Quick, back into your tunnel until we disembark."

The next wonderful sound to my ears was the stopping of the engines and the squeaking and groaning of the huge bumpers cushioning the ship against the dock. At least an hour went by before the deck hatches opened for the unloading of the cargo. I began to worry a bit at this point, but not for long. Rick ran over and called me to follow him on the double. I lost little time in following his orders. The boys shuffled me back and forth in their cabins until the customs inspection was over. Now it was time for liberty. My garb was similar to that of a deckhand going on shore leave. There was no uniform to worry about on this tramp steamer.

"OK, Ron, come on. Follow me," ordered Rick. I found myself between Rick and Krieger. For the first time in over two weeks I was topside. The air smelled pure, clean, and free. We walked along the starboard side, past the quarter deck and onto the gangplank. Rick and Krieger made so much racket whooping it up and giving a half-salute to the Officer of the Deck, that the guard hardly noticed me as I walked off the gangplank. As soon as my feet touched terra firma, I was overwhelmed with the realization that I was now standing on the free soil of Great Britain. I didn't realize that there were tears on my cheeks until Krieger grabbed me by the elbow and hurried me along.

"What is this?" he asked. "I thought Legionnaires were tough."

"You are talking to one who is definitely an ex-Legionnaire." I said. We entered the nearest pub and took a table in the corner. Over glasses of stout we made our final plans.

"How much money do you have, Ron?" asked Rick.

"I've got nine thousand Algerian francs. Find me a bank and we can exchange it for English money."

"No, Ron," said Rick. "It will take days for the bank to make the transaction. There isn't that much time. Tell you what, swabs, what say we each toss in a pound or so to make Ron's fare to England? There he can change his francs to English pounds."

"Look men, you have done more than enough already," I protested. "You saved my life. I couldn't possibly take your money after what you did for me."

"Enough." scowled Krieger with a half-grin. "Here is enough money to get to England. Someday you can post it to us if you feel you have to." I pocketed the money and shook hands with my friends. After a final toast I went to the bus station and bought a ticket to Edinburgh.

"Wait up, Reynolds," shouted Rick. I'm going to Edinburgh too."

"Great, Rick. Then you can help me get a ticket to England. Any suggestions?"

"How does this sound? From Edinburgh we take a train to Manchester, my home town. I have a few days off and you can stay with my family while you make arrangements to get home.

"Now wait a minute," I said. "Enough is enough. You keep doing too much for me."

"You are still taking orders from me, that is final. Come on, let's get on that bus." During the trip Rick persuaded me to stay with him while working things out.

"Say, Ron, 1957 is almost over," he remarked. "Late November is a special occasion in your country, isn't it?"

"Well I'll be damned. I almost forgot about Thanksgiving. I sure have a lot to give thanks for this year."

Then we pulled into Manchester Rick said, "Here we are. You are about to have the best meal you've had in eighteen months. After you get squared away we'll get in touch with the American Embassy."

Rick's family welcomed me with open arms. They were working class and good-hearted. Rick had several brothers and sisters, and they all worked as laborers, bus drivers, or in factories. Their brownstone type row house was furnished with old furniture. These were people with big hearts, all of them. My first night at Rick's was the first chance I had to write to my parents since my escape.

Manchester, England
November 28, 1957

Dear Mom and Dad,

This may come as a surprise to you, but I am a free man again. God has heard your plea on my behalf and thus shown me His mercy, for which I will be grateful for as long as I live.

After escaping that living hell, I feel like a new person. I think life could not appear sweeter. At times when I am walking down a street I experience such beautiful elation and throb of life, that I feared it might not be true and have pinched myself to make sure. If anyone can grasp the meaning to these feelings, they would be you. You'll never know the kindness I've found in some of the people over here. I am safe and well, living with the family of one of my rescuers. I will explain in detail about my escape when I get home. I will need passage home, and it can be sent to me in care of Rick's address. I plan to consult with the American Consul tomorrow. I will try and be home with you as soon as I manage to find a way.

Please don't worry Mom and Dad. I feel wonderful. The only thing left is to be with you both again.

Your loving son,
Ronnie

Ron's passport to freedom was the British steamer
USMOUTH, which was docked at Oran.

Three British seamen who smuggled Ron aboard
their ship and kept him safely hidden

CHAPTER 23

It took several days before Mr. Sharkly of the Consulate could cut enough red tape to secure me a passage on an airliner headed for New York City. Money from home arrived just in time. Rick's mother and sisters hugged and kissed me goodbye, and I shook hands with Rick, his father, and his brothers. Rick gave me a pair of dungarees and a black T-shirt. A friend of one of Rick's brothers gave me a pair of shoes to replace my old sandals. People were sure good to me. As the Consul's car took me from Rick's home to the airport, I looked out the window. In spite of the fact that I was finally going home, I felt a bit sad saying goodbye to my friend, Rick. Mr. Sharkly broke the silence.

"Well, pretty soon you will be back home where you belong. I don't think I have lecture you on the foolish decision you made to join the French Foreign Legion. I believe you have more than learned your lesson. Things won't be easy for you when you get back into civilian life. You still are a man without a country and will have to wait five years like any other alien before getting back your citizenship. You can thank your parents and Congressman for rushing through an emergency visa for you. Personally, I was a bit miffed when you first contacted me. I felt that you could have at least joined one of our armed services if it was action you were after. I realize now that you acted hastily in a quest for glamour and adventure. How do you feel now?"

"Believe me, Mr. Sharkly, I am the first to admit I made a terrible mistake. I learned a lot the hard way. I learned that the French army is contemptuous of Americans. They use American weapons, but they think we are foolish to sell or give them to a foreign country. The French have a good thing in the Legion. They don't use their own men to fight. They don't even have to use their own weapons. The mercenaries get colonies for France and keep the natives down. My conscience doesn't bother me because I deserted. I joined the Legion to become a soldier, not an animal. However, it is something to be proud of to have been in the Legion. The Legion is the toughest fighting force in the world, maybe because a Legionnaire has nothing to live for."

"I think I understand. I'm glad I can help you get home."

After we got to the airport I picked up all of my worldly possessions, which half-filled a small paper bag. My passage through customs was cleared ahead of time. The Consul had taken care of it. He also had wired my folks, telling them what time my plane was due at La Guardia Airport, and the time of transfer to a Buffalo bound plane and its estimated time of arrival.

The lights of New York City at night were never more beautiful than that early December evening. When I stepped off the plane I was thinking of the old newsreels which showed homecoming servicemen dropping to their knees and kissing the good old U.S. ground. I touched my fingers to my lips, then bent down and placed them on the ground. I was home, and my ordeal as a lost soul was over.

I rushed into the terminal and to the ticket counter to buy the ticket which would take me on the last leg home. It was then that I received another jolt. Every bit of cash on my person was in English money. Not only was I unable to purchase a flight to Buffalo, but I had no American currency for room, meals or a phone call home. In my state of confusion, I never thought of reversing the charges. Like an animal in shock I walked the streets of New York the entire night until the banks opened the next day and I could exchange my money. Adding to my troubles was a subway strike in the city.

I finally made my way to a bank, redeemed my money and took a bus to Buffalo.

It was late in the evening, but my home was all lit up. I just stood in front and took in the beautiful sight as light snow flakes floated gently by. The door was unlocked, as usual. I don't think we ever had a key to our house. I walked into the front hall. My father was on the telephone talking to someone in New York concerning my flight. Standing next to him with her hands together was Mother. And seated on a nearby couch with her legs folded under her was my sister. All three looked up at the same time. Then there was one hell of a scream. Dad dropped the phone, and all three came running over to me. Before they reached me I glanced at the two vigil lights burning in the hall before the statue of the Blessed Virgin Mary, fell to my knees and gave thanks for my safe return. I had a tough time getting to my feet with the kisses and hugs of Mom and Sue, and the back-thumping of Dad.

"Ronnie!" screamed Mom, "Where have you been? We wondered what happened to you."

Sue chimed in. "You big nut, it's good to see you. We thought the French caught up with you and shipped you back."

Then it was Dad's turn. "Son, good to have you back. I was just talking to New York. We had a search going. Even the FBI was notified."

"Well I'm here now and I'm okay. No more worrying. Anything left over from supper?"

Mom looked me over and said, "Oh Ron, how thin you are. They couldn't have fed you in that horrible Legion."

Sue added, "Why he speaks with a French accent. And he only had two years of it in high school."

Dad took over. "Well, that's all over with. Now let's all sit down and bring each other up to date. Then it's a home-cooked meal for you, a nice hot bath, and a clean comfortable bed."

The Legion was never like this...my family, loving care, good chow, and a bath with hot water. In a few days the holiday season would begin. What a contrast to the previous Christmas in the prison dungeon with the sadistic Turk. I had to erase these nightmares from my mind now. I hope they will stay away. For the first time in a year and a half I was able to kneel before my bed before retiring, to thank God for His Mercy in seeing me through my ordeal. I was home again.

THE END

Fran Lucca..Retired Print, Wire Service and Broadcast Investigative Reporter and 1999 Inductee into the Buffalo Broadcasters Hall of Fame. He and his wife Mary Jane live in Buffalo, N.Y.

Printed in the United States
By Bookmasters